MICHAEL BROADBENT'S
POCKET GUIDE TO
WINE VINTAGES

A Fireside Book

Published by Simon & Schuster Inc.
NEW YORK   LONDON   TORONTO   SYDNEY
TOKYO   SINGAPORE

A Fireside Book
Published by Simon & Schuster Inc
Simon & Schuster Building
Rockefeller Center
1230 Avenue of the Americas
New York, NY 10020

Copyright © 1992 by Mitchell Beazley International Ltd

Executive Editor: Anne Ryland
Editors: Elizabeth Bellord, Susan Keevil
Art Director: Tim Foster
Art Editor: Rozelle Bentheim
Production: Sarah Schuman
Film by Tradespools Ltd, Frome, Somerset
Printed and bound in Great Britain by
HarperCollins Manufacturing, Glasgow

10 9 8 7 6 5 4 3 2 1

Library of Congress Cataloging in Publication Data

Broadbent, Michael.
    [Pocket guide to wine vintages]
    Michael Broadbent's pocket guide to wine vintages / Michael
Broadbent.
       p.   cm.
    "A Fireside book."
    "A Mitchell Beazley book" -- T.p. verso.
    "First published in Great Britain in 1992 by Mitchell Beazley
Publishers ... London" -- T.p. verso.
    ISBN 0-671-74215-9 : $11.95
    1. Wine and wine making.   I. Title. II. Title: Pocket guide to
wine vintages.
TP548.B852 1992
841.2'2--dc20   92-4685
                                                             CIP

ISBN: 0-671-74215-9

CONTENTS

FOREWORD

The purpose of this new pocketbook is to answer two basic questions: 'what is a vintage?' and 'why are vintages important?' and then to rate every significant vintage of all the world's principal wine districts and wine types, assessing quality, advising whether, and for how long, one should keep young wine, and summarising the maturity and current drinkability of the wines of former vintages.

The main text, arranged by district and type of wine, listing up to a century of vintage years, goes far beyond the familiar vintage charts both in range and scope, and explains briefly the conditions which produced the good, bad and indifferent vintages and wines. Yet the handy pocketbook format will, I trust, make it both a practical and convenient work of reference.

Michael Broadbent
Christie's, London, Summer 1992

INTRODUCTION

WINE, THE OLDEST, MOST NATURAL AND HEALTHIEST of beverages, is the combined product of nature and man. It is part natural, part man-made. Vines are planted and tended. They produce an annual crop of grapes which, after harvesting, is fermented into wine. Nature produces, man guides.

Unlike most other agricultural products, soft fruits for example, wine is to a certain extent manufactured, its natural fermentation controlled. Its 'shelf life' is as varied as its colour, smell and taste. Grapes for the making of good wine can only be grown in a temperate climate, the basic differences of type being due to the variety of vine cultivated, the soil, subsoil, aspect and drainage. Once the vineyard is planted these elements are to a certain extent 'fixed'.

Thereafter the hand of man, his skill in tending the vines and of winemaking, introduces a controllable variable. The other variable, more or less beyond man's control, is the weather. The weather is the key to the vintage.

WHAT IS A 'VINTAGE'?

The word vintage has two meanings. 'The vintage' is the time of grape harvesting, 'vintaging', less often used, refers simply to the picking of grapes at harvest time, that short or extended period in the autumn which follows the growing and ripening season, when – all being well – the grapes are at their optimum state of maturity with the desired levels of grape sugar, acidity and other component parts.

The growing and ripening season is annual which means that there is a vintage every year: every wine, strictly speaking, is therefore a vintage wine. Whether it remains so depends on its quality, the best being nursed and nurtured to retain its individuality. In practice a high proportion of the world's annual production of wines loses its vintage identity shortly after it is made as it is blended either with other wine made in the same year or with vatted wines of previous vintages. Examples of the latter are sherry and 'wood port'.

In the broader context, however, the term 'vintage' in relation to wine has an implied quality connotation, not necessarily good, but sometimes most specifically so, as in the case of vintage port and vintage champagne.

WHY ARE VINTAGES IMPORTANT?

The producer of fine wine, the importer, merchant, investor and consumer is acutely conscious of vintages. They have a direct bearing on the value of the wine, whether youthful and immature or old and mature. For the connoisseur vintages provide an endless fascination, their nuances noted, understood, appreciated.

The value of a vintage wine is directly proportional to its perceived quality, though the price demanded at source, or paid on the open market, is greatly enhanced by its scarcity value – where production is small (for example Château Pétrus, a small vineyard compared to the first-growths of the Médoc; also the world demand for the minute supply of Romanée-Conti and Le Montrachet) or where availability of a great, mature and mostly consumed vintage is limited (for example Château Mouton-Rothschild 1945 or Château d'Yquem 1921).

That poorer vintages of the wine of great estates command lower prices than those of the best vintages is amply borne out by prices in the London salesrooms. For example the 1968 vintage of Château Lafite sells for roughly one-eighth the price of the 1959, the 1963 one-sixteenth that of the 1961.

Quite apart from price, there is the important matter of how good the wine is as a drink: its unready immaturity, its agreeable young fruit, the perfection of one carefully cellared and perfectly developed, its balance of component parts, its harmony, its imbalance, over-acidity, and so forth: all are functions of vintage.

In short vintages vary, and a knowledge and understanding of this is an important part of wine appreciation.

WHAT MAKES A GOOD OR A BAD VINTAGE?

Given the fixed elements of temperate climate, soils, vine stocks, and winemaking traditions and techniques, the joker in the pack is the weather. No matter where in the world vines are grown, all are subject to variations of weather conditions during the grape growing and ripening season which vary from minor and subtle to dramatic and highly significant. Growers can do little except take evasive action, by no means always effective. The timing and permutations of cold, heat, dryness, rain, sunshine, lack of sun, and humidity have a direct bearing on the eventual quality of grapes and of the style and quality of the wine made. Rather like the human face, none is identical despite the commonality of eyes, nose, mouth, hair etc; the vine's growing season has bud-break, flowering, grape set, ripening – yet no one year is alike another.

Whether the vineyard is a small holding managed by a part-time farmer who has a job in town, a major full-time family operation, a managed estate, or vast rolling acres of vines owned by a multinational, the basic elements of vine husbandry are the same. The vine management season begins soon after the annual grape harvest.

Late autumn/winter After the harvest, long shoots are removed, and ploughing between rows is carried out to cover the base of the vinestocks as a protection against severe chill and frosts. Pruning can start from mid-December (for simplicity I am assuming that the vineyard is in the northern hemisphere). A cold winter is good for the vines. They are dormant, resting after the exertions of the previous season and harvest. The bigger and better the crop, the greater need for rest.

New year and spring Pruning continues until early March when the sap starts to rise. The winter covering of the vines is reversed, the soil being removed from their base. This period can be one of happy anticipation or worry. If too mild, the vegetation is advanced, and the likelihood of frost-damage far increased. Just one frost in April or early May can wreak havoc, critically reducing the potential crop (as was the case in 1991, the new shoots being literally nipped in the bud) or, if severe, can even destroy the vines.

Action can be taken as a precaution against frosts – 'smudge pots', stoves in the vineyard, wind machines – but can be expensive and often ineffective. Though a severe frost will be crippling it can also have a beneficial outcome, for what is in effect a drastic pruning results in a small crop which, if the summer is hot and dry, can lead to concentrated, high quality grapes – as was the case in 1945 and 1961 in Bordeaux.

Late spring, early summer Let us assume that there has been no crippling frost. Weeds are cleared and vines are sprayed with fungicides to prevent two potentially leaf damaging diseases, oidium and mildew. The next period is also crucial: the flowering of the vine. Ideal conditions are warm and dry so that the flowering takes place early and over a short period. The earlier the flowering the sooner the vintage. If the weather is cold and wet, flowering is delayed and prolonged, resulting in failure to pollinate (*coulure*): the embryo grapes do not develop, and eventually fall off.

Another problem is partial pollination (*millerandage*), resulting in tiny seedless berries which, though usually very sweet, reduce the volume of grape juice.

As a rule of thumb the vines need 100 days of sun between flowering and picking. The later the flowering the later – and generally the more risky – the harvest.

Shoots are thinned. More spraying is carried out if necessary.

Mid- to late summer Ideally, what is needed is a judicious mixture of warm sunshine and light rain, the one to bring on the ripening, the other to swell the berries.

August can be uneventful. There is more thinning and weeding as the grapes change colour (*veraison*). In particularly good years with potentially bountiful crops, some growers in the best vineyards 'green prune', cutting off whole bunches to reduce quantities, nourishment from the soil is then concentrated in fewer grapes. This is an expensive process and only justified if the increase of quality is matched by a satisfactory price for the wine.

Early autumn If the spring and early summer – bud formation and flowering – are responsible for the potential size of the crop and earliest possible date of picking, the very late summer and early autumn ripening period is responsible for the creation of adequate sugar content and richness of component parts. The balance of acidity and sugar is important. The riper the grapes, the higher the sugar content and the stronger the alcohol after fermentation. But as grapes ripen beyond a certain stage the level of acidity is reduced. Acidity is vital for the life, vigour, refreshing quality and longevity of the wine. I personally think of acidity – tartaric, the grape acid – as the nervous system of the wine. Conversely, unripe grapes have too little natural sugar and an insufficiency of potential alcohol, a situation which can be remedied, if officially sanctioned, by the addition of cane sugar to the grape juice or must prior to fermentation. In unripe grapes, acidity tends to be high and of the wrong sort: malic acid, which is tart, like cooking apples.

The harvest – 'the vintage' – itself takes place when the grapes have achieved optimum ripeness and before the cold weather sets in. In Bordeaux mid-September is considered early, the end of September usually satisfactory, early October not abnormal, but later is risky. After exceptionally hot summers the picking of white grapes for dry wine can start in August, though this very rarely happens for reds. The grapes for naturally sweet wines made in classic districts like Sauternes and in Germany will generally be picked later than those for the dry whites and reds to obtain the extra ripeness.

Destalking and fermentation – in short winemaking – are man-controlled operations, and depend on the whim and expertise of the owner or oenologist, on local practices, and on the style and quality of wine aimed for. The differences are important but are either predictable, because the methods are well tried and known, or can be ascertained.

The only unpredictable variable is the weather. This, I stress again, is what makes vintages important.

POSTSCRIPT

It is often said that good wines can be made in bad vintages just as bad wines can be made in good vintages. This is a half-truism. Mistakes, carelessness, sheer ineptness can spoil a potentially good wine. Conversely, a skilled and conscientious vine-grower and winemaker can mollify disasters, making the best wine that inclement weather will allow. But in the final analysis, good wine can only be made from good grapes, and good grapes can only be grown in suitable weather conditions.

STAR RATING

★★★★★	Outstanding (vintage or wine)
★★★★	Very good
★★★	Good
★★	Moderately good
★	Not very good, but not bad
No stars/~	Poor

ACKNOWLEGEMENTS

Australian Wine Board
Vicky Bishop (New Zealand Wine Guild)
Peter Cobb
Columbia Winery
Comité Interprofessionnel du Vin de Champagne (CIVC)
Decanter Magazine
Peter Devereux
Eyrie Vineyard
Alberto Fornos
Gabor Egressy
James Halliday
Alex Hargrave
Lindemans Wines Ltd

The Madeira Wine Company Lda
Richard Mayson
Mondavi Winery
The New York Grape Foundation
Penfolds Wines Ltd
John Platter
Bernard L Rhodes MD
Peter A Sichel
Simi Winery
James Symington
Miguel Torres
Rebecca Wasserman
Andrew Williams
Wines from Spain
Yarra Yering Wines Ltd

BORDEAUX

BORDEAUX, ONE OF THE OLDEST, LARGEST AND most famous classic wine regions of the world, is situated in the southwest of France. The various districts which radiate from its hub, the surprisingly big and now sprawling city and port, produce a vast quantity of red wine ranging in quality from everyday to the finest, a substantial volume of dry white, some of the highest quality, and sweet white wine from the merely pleasant to the sublime.

Bordeaux has a maritime climate, temperate and perfect for vine growing. However, rather like an island, the weather throughout the growing season is subject to manifold changes, some minor and subtle, others major and crucial: conditions that effect the timing and success of the budding of the vine, its flowering, ripening and harvest. In short, each season has its variations, resulting in wines of different style, weight and quality. Here, as elsewhere, the vineyard manager must tend his vines, cope with the exigencies of weather and take evasive action against pests and diseases; the *maître de chai* and oenologist must make the best of the grapes harvested. The wines of Bordeaux are an infinite challenge for producer, broker, *négociant*, importer, merchant and, perhaps most important of all, the consumer.

RED BORDEAUX

ONE OF THE MOST IMPORTANT AND SIGNIFICANT differences between red Bordeaux and red wine of many other classic districts is that it is made not from just one major vine variety, but several, each with different characteristics; the choice between them being dictated by the soil type which, again, varies throughout the region, and the style of wine aimed for. Moreover, each grape variety has, in effect, its own life style: Merlot, for example, is an early ripener, susceptible to rot, and the small-berried Cabernet Sauvignon is firmer and ripens later. The latter grape has the strongest association with Bordeaux, the proportion cultivated usually being by far the highest, certainly the most dominant, in the Médoc and Graves, yet rarely planted in the Pomerol and St-Emilion districts where Merlot is favoured. Cabernet Franc is a major partner to the Merlot in these hillier districts to the north and east of Bordeaux, but is just one of the supporting cast of grapes in the Médoc. Other varieties, notably Petit Verdot, are grown but only as a small proportion, two to five percent, of the varietal or *cépage* mix, if at all.

The importance of these different grape varieties is that in juxtaposition they provide the correct balance of component parts to create red Bordeaux. To a lesser extent they are a sort of insurance: if the Merlot fails the Cabernet Sauvignon and Franc might well survive for the winemaker to use; if the Merlot is ripe but the weather deteriorates and the Cabernets fail to ripen, a Merlot dominated wine will be made.

It is these infinite variations, of *cépage* mix, of age and maturity, of soils and subsoils, of literally thousands of individual vineyards, of weather throughout the growing season, and of the subtle manifestations of change as the wine matures, first in cask then in bottle, that make red Bordeaux – claret – so endlessly fascinating. A kaleidoscope, warranting a life-time's study; an endless challenge, affording endless enjoyment.

A word of warning: it is not possible in a paragraph to sum up the characteristics of the wines of every district, let alone of individual châteaux. Though the overall weather pattern in a given year is common to all, microclimates do exist, and vine growers and winemakers are only human.

Lastly, a word about longevity. Only major châteaux, the classed growths and their equivalents, with vines on prime sites, are capable of producing true *vin de garde* wines which will not only keep but improve with bottle-age. Minor wines from less favoured vineyard sites and districts will, in a good vintage, keep but they will not necessarily improve: softening a little perhaps, but not developing the richness of bouquet, the extra dimensions of flavour and refinement of the great growths. Bourgeois claret is best drunk between three and eight years of age, depending on the vintage, whereas classed growths need, in a good vintage, from six to 15 years, great wines in great vintages keeping and improving for over 20 years.

1991★★ to ★★★

An uneven year. Small production due to severe spring frosts. A vintage that veered from disaster to the verge of great success but did not, in the end, make it. Certainly nothing like the overall quality of the preceding three vintages. What caused the problems? As usual the main culprit was the weather.

The winter of 1990 was very wet; December cold yet ending with a record 19.5°C (67°F) on the 29th. January was very dry, with eight days of frost and two of snow; February was also very dry, with five days of snow, during which time the vines were dormant. March was dry and mild, encouraging growth; April, until the 17th, was mild with average rainfall and a little hail: vegetation advancing satisfactorily.

On the night of April 21/22 the temperature plummeted to as low as –8°C (18°F). Vines were frozen, new shoots destroyed overnight, and the potential crop decimated. The cold weather continued, warming up as May progressed, with average rainfall. June was unsettled, the first ten days wet, the last ten days dry. Consequently flowering, from around June 15 to early July, was late, prolonged and uneven. There were early signs of mildew and grape worm.

July was hot, with above average rainfall which caused more worries about rot. August was dry and hot, in fact the hottest August since 1926. Above-average temperatures continued into September, advancing ripening and encouraging some growers, particularly in the Médoc, to anticipate another high quality, small, concentrated crop like 1961. However, the riper the grapes the greater the rot problems. The *coup de grâce* was delivered towards the end of the month, with eight days of rain prior to harvesting. Those whose vines had survived the big frost had now to sort out the ripe from rotten grapes, this separation being crucial for quality.

Despite these vicissitudes some good wines were made, particularly in the more favoured areas of the Médoc. The surviving grapes were fully ripe, had excellent acidity and good soft tannins, the Merlot attaining the best sugar levels. Some proprietors anticipate quality superior to 1981, possibly on a par with 1962, even 1985. But throughout the region the crop was small, the worst off being St-Emilion, the production of some châteaux being down to 10% of normal.

As always, the minor reds can and should be drunk young –

between three and five years after the vintage. Too early to assess the keeping qualities of the great growths and, to be frank, there is no need to rush into them with such excellent and predictable vintages preceding.

1990★★★★

A large and successful vintage. It is very rare, indeed unprecedented, to have three successive vintages of the quality of 1988, 1989 and 1990.

January to March was unusually warm, resulting in an early budding, but progress slowed during a cold, frosty patch in late March and early April. Beneficial rain in April was followed by a very hot, dry, sunny May. A second spurt of growth resulted in unevenness in the vines in some parts of Bordeaux, there were particular variations between the Merlot and Cabernet Sauvignon.

Hot, sunny weather lasted until the end of August but, despite the heat and drought, ripening was excellent. Happily, gentle rainfall saved the day, swelling and ripening the grapes and giving colour to the skins. Picking only became general in mid-September. The best grapes came from estates where the bunches had been carefully thinned. The Merlot grapes were in excellent condition with some of the highest sugar levels ever recorded. The Cabernet Sauvignon grapes, however, had had a difficult, prolonged flowering and the berries tended to be small and thick, prompting fears that the wines from the Médoc would be inferior to those from St-Emilion and Pomerol where the Merlot dominates.

Overall, this was an abundant, exciting vintage, particularly for the Merlots which have enormous amounts of tannin. The best Cabernet Sauvignons were made where the growers held out before picking; they had enough acidity to balance the slightly low acid content of the Merlot. Overall, well-constituted, fairly powerful wines. The best may well be the *cru bourgeois* rather than the second growths.

Minor wines from lesser districts will be attractive to drink whilst still young and fruity; good quality St-Emilion and Pomerol from 1995–2000, and the classed growth Médocs from 1996–2015, the best far beyond.

1989★★★★★

An extremely attractive vintage following an exceptionally hot summer – the hottest since 1949 – which produced wines of real promise, though not without a few problems along the way.

By May, growth was already three weeks ahead of normal. Early flowering in excellent conditions ensured a substantially sized crop. The hot weather continued through to September with uneven, but surprisingly good, levels of rainfall. Picking began on August 28 – the earliest harvest since 1893.

Growers in the Merlot-dominated vineyards of the right bank found that the grapes, though technically ripe, did not have ripe tannins; where tannins were allowed to ripen, the acidity level dropped. Problems were further compounded throughout Bordeaux by the high sugar levels, which contributed to fermentation difficulties.

Despite the problems more familiar to the New World than to southwestern France, these are rich, ripe wines with luscious fruit and good tannin levels. The '89s bear comparison in many respects with the '85s, perhaps richer overall.

An extremely attractive vintage, full of fruit and charm. Virtually all will be precociously drinkable, but under that appealing 'puppy fat' have the component parts to ensure good development and, for the top growths, a fairly long life, well into the 21st century.

1988★★★★

Undoubtedly an excellent vintage – particularly from those estates where the growers nervously sat out the late-September storms and harvested the grapes in an exceptionally warm, sunny October.

A mild, wet winter and spring necessitated widespread spraying and resulted in an uneven flowering. This was followed by a hot, dry summer which lasted right through from July until September.

The dry summer produced wines with great depth of colour and high levels of tannin, especially in the Merlot-dominated vineyards of the right bank. Where the grapes were picked late, the tannin was complemented by good levels of fruit.

A firm, well-structured vintage, suitable for laying down; not as immediately charming as 1989 but capable of longer life.

Classed growth Médocs not before 1995; they will mature well into the 21st century. The best Graves, Pomerols and St-Emilions from the late 1990s to around 2010.

1987★★

This year suffers from comparison with the two good vintages it followed – and the three it preceded. However, these were, on balance, light, attractive wines throughout Bordeaux, suitable for early drinking.

A long cold winter and spring followed by a cool, humid June, resulted in prolonged and uneven flowering. A relatively cool and dull July and August, thereafter, apart from some rain in early September, the weather was generally fine, hot sun being succeeded by an unsettled October, the grapes being harvested in dull and rainy conditions.

1987 yielded an average sized crop of sound wines. Overall, a useful stop-gap vintage, providing pleasant drinking while the more important vintages, the '86s and '88s, and younger wines are maturing.

Even the top growths can – should – be drunk soon, say now–1998. All the rest, drink up – certainly before 1997.

1986★★★★

The biggest crop since World War II: 15% larger than that of the 1985 vintage.

A cool, damp spring delayed bud-break, but the weather improved during May and June. After a successful flowering, the summer was hot and dry until the harvest, which began during the last week in September.

The size of the crop provoked some worries about its quality. These are, however, intense, powerful, tannic wines and those with sufficient extract and flesh will last well.

Try and leave the first-growths until after 2000. Other classed growths will be ready sooner, say from the mid–1990s, and those of bourgeois quality are drinking quite well now.

1985★★★★★

Very appealing wines produced after a growing season veering from one extreme to the other. The winter was one of the coldest on record, and caused considerable frost damage in some areas.

A very good, very early flowering took place at the beginning of a long, extremely hot summer. The hot, dry weather held right up until the harvest, which took place in ideal conditions in late September/early October.

The '85s combine high quantity with high quality. The wines are ripe, opulent and luscious with soft fruit. Some lesser areas showed a tendency to overproduce, resulting in slightly diluted wines. Overall, however, beautifully-balanced claret.

Misleadingly attractive to drink now yet the best should be kept and will continue to evolve to 2010 and beyond. The lesser wines might as well be drunk whilst relatively young and fruity.

1984★

Difficult weather conditions, including the arrival of Hurricane Hortense on October 5, resulted in variable wines.

After a cold February and March, conditions improved with a warm April. The cold weather returned in May and an incomplete flowering took place during an excessively hot, dry June. The summer was fair, followed by a humid September and wet October. Picking began in late September/early October, and was interrupted by the hurricane.

Merlot vines suffered from *coulure*, reducing the crop drastically. There were, therefore, few wines of quality from the right bank. In the Médoc the wines are virtually all Cabernet.

The 1984 vintage does not compare well with other excellent vintages of the same period; they are lean, hard, ungracious wines which also suffered from over-pricing, making them, in some instances, more expensive than the superior '83s and '82s.

My advice: drink soon. The best will not improve much, nor will the minor wines soften.

1983★★★

A large crop of good quality, which produced some very appealing wines, more typical of Bordeaux than the '82s.

After a poor start to the year conditions improved in time for the flowering, and the summer was hot and dry. Graves experienced hail during early July and other areas suffered disease due to excessive humidity; but the harvest, which began September 26, took place in ideal conditions. Margaux was the most favoured district. Right bank wine was generally less fine.

These wines have a good balance of tannin, fruit and acidity and are ageing reasonably well. The '83s do, however, lack the opulence of the '82s and are not as well-constructed or well-balanced as the '85s.

Virtually all are drinking well now though the better Médocs will continue to develop, some even beyond 2000.

1982★★★★★

An exceptional vintage throughout Bordeaux – the '82s were immediately perceived as a potential 'vintage of the decade'.

Not, however, typical Bordeaux: described by some as more like California Cabernet than claret.

Flowering was early and even. The climate provided ideal growing conditions for the vines. Consistently hot, dry weather held throughout the summer, though some areas in the Médoc and Graves experiencing a hot, stormy July.

The harvest started on September 14 in perfect conditions. A large crop of exceptionally ripe grapes was gathered, causing some concern that the wines would not, as a result, have the necessary structure to mature into good claret.

The results, however, are huge, opulent, luscious wines with high extract masking considerable tannin content, which will take some time to mature.

The top wines of the Médoc might well go through an extended period of seemingly little development but should prove magnificently rich and long-term. Most Pomerols, St-Emilions and red Graves are drinking well now but will keep. Minor wines: drink whilst the young fruit is still evident.

1981★★ to ★★★★

A small crop of good quality wines. This vintage has been overshadowed by the more immediately impressive '82s, and by other successful vintages of the 1980s.

Flowering took place early in hot, dry weather which held throughout the summer. September saw some gentle rain which cleared up in time for the harvest, which began on October 1. Some skinny wines not worth pursuing, but many others are well-constituted and merit keeping.

More of a claret man's claret than the '82 and, on the whole, drinking well. The top growths should improve, soften, though most are on the lean side. Some particularly good Pomerols. Minor wines: drink soon.

1980★

With the odd exception, this is an average vintage which, like 1981, has suffered in comparison to the high quality of most of the other 1980s vintages.

A cool spring resulted in a late and uneven flowering; June was consistently cold and wet, followed by a moderate summer. Grapes ripened very slowly, necessitating a delayed harvest – picking started as late as October 20 in some areas.

These were 'lunchtime' clarets, ideal for early drinking. While it is unlikely that any will age particularly well, this was a useful and surprisingly attractive vintage.

Drinking now: with few exceptions prior to the mid-1990s.

1979★★

Abundant: the biggest harvest since 1934. Initially unwanted, upstaged by the '78s, '79s began to be appreciated in the mid-to-late 1980s. They have now been overtaken by the better wines of the 1980s decade.

A cold wet spring, which followed a hard winter, delayed bud-break until mid-April, but the summer was fine apart from a cold spell in August. The harvest took place in good conditions in mid-October: a very large crop of small, thick-skinned grapes, lacking full ripeness and resulting in deep-coloured, tannic wines.

The right bank vineyards – St-Emilion and Pomerol – had a very successful year, with a fine, ripe crop adding a more luscious note to the vintage.

The right bank wines are delicious now but there is a risk that the more tannic Médocs will dry out, lacking sufficient fruit. Though many will keep, relatively few will improve.

1978★★★

The year described by Harry Waugh, director of Château Latour, as 'the year of the miracle': appalling growing conditions saved by perfect early autumn weather.

The spring was late, with bud-break and harvest delayed a little. But after the late grape set in mid-August conditions improved, ripening taking place in unbroken sunshine until the start of the harvest on October 9. At some properties picking continued into late October.

The vintage was well received for several reasons: it turned out far better than originally feared; the '77s were poor, the market was right.

I think that this vintage has been overrated and is on the decline. A good proportion of the wines are drinking well but I doubt if many will improve. Drink soon.

1977

A poor vintage, the worst of an uneven decade. An early bud-break was damaged by spring frosts, then rain throughout the summer was followed by the driest September since 1851 which saved the crop from complete disaster. The wines were generally unexciting, colour was sometimes good but most lacked length and depth. The best showed a specious chap-talised fruitiness which soon wore off.

Drink up.

1976★★ to ★★★★

A deservedly popular vintage. A year of exceptional heat in northwest Europe, Bordeaux included, with a summer-long drought that broke during the harvest.

The bud-break was at the normal time, during late March, with flowering, grape set and vintage all early as the heat carried out its work. Picking started on September 15, the earliest of the decade.

The wines turned out to be easy and agreeable, but many, from high to low class, lack flesh; more lean and supple than pleasantly fresh. 1976 provided a good crop of 'luncheon claret' at the middle level, while some of the first-growths have surprised with their concentration and elegance.

Never a classic claret vintage, though some tasters were misled by its youthful appeal, attractive colour and initial fruit.

Some continue to charm and delight. Most are flavoury but fading. One or two top growths have time in hand. On balance: drink up.

1975★ to ★★★★

Following three mediocre, graceless vintages, this was unhesitatingly pronounced a *vin de garde* by the Bordelaise, but, despite its undoubted richness, its future is uncertain.

A mild, wet winter, followed by a mild spring with occasional frosts, provided favourable conditions for flowering. The summer was hot and dry with some gentle, welcome rain before the harvest (beginning on September 26), which was generally dry except for a few hailstorms.

Fruity wines with a dark colour resulting from a deep pigment in the grape skins; a high sugar content, assured a satisfactory alcohol level. However, despite good fruit and high extract, the tannins seem excessive: many wines have a 'rusty' orange tinge, misleadingly mature-looking but still with a swingeingly dry, tannic finish.

The most difficult of all recent vintages to assess and predict. Some are rich and delicious, and the best-endowed will doubtless keep. Some, however, are drying out. Time will tell.

1974

A very large, unwelcome vintage at a time of slump in Bordeaux. Good flowering weather; hot summer followed by a wet and increasingly cold autumn. Picking began on October 3. Overall raw, ungracious wines.

Drink up.

1973★★

An enormous vintage of light, at best modestly attractive wines, which coincided with the severe recession in the wine market.

Fine weather all summer except for a very wet July. Vintage started on October 1 under satisfactory conditions, yielding a huge crop. The majority of wines lacked colour, substance and charm. Had the market been more propitious it might have paid the growers to prune harder and be more selective: better wines would have resulted.

Drink now. Some can be surprisingly pleasing.

1972

One of the latest vintages since records began. Overpricing of these poor wines triggered the collapse of the Bordeaux market.

A fairly large crop of immature, uneven quality grapes. Dismal but not undrinkable wines were made: unwanted and, latterly, cheap.

Drink up, or avoid.

1971★★★★

A good vintage with some elegant wines, though yields were much lower than in previous years. A cold, wet spring and early summer followed by warm and sunny weather with light rain – an ideal combination. Picking started on October 4.

The Pomerols were outstanding and some Médocs excellent.

Many pleasant surprises though some of the top Médocs are a bit lean. Many red Graves, Pomerols and St-Emilions are delicious now but should continue to please towards the end of the century.

1970★★★★

An imposing vintage which combined quantity with high quality, though, in my opinion, possibly not as uniformly excellent as the 1966.

Spring was late but the vines blossomed in good conditions. July's great heat and drought was followed by a rainy, cooler August with hot intervals. September began stormy and cold, but soon gave way to a long run of hot sunshine throughout the vintage which started on October 4.

One notable result of these weather conditions was that all the main grape varieties, Cabernet Sauvignon, Cabernet Franc, Merlot and even Petit Verdot ripened fully and simultaneously. Some disappointments, particularly in the Médoc but overall still impressive.

Many of the top Pomerols and St-Emilions are perfection now but will keep. However, many of the well-constituted wines of the Médoc have been going through a rather long drawn-out, unyielding period; bearing in mind their composition though, I believe that the best will eventually open up, even if one has to wait until after 2000.

1969★

Unappealing, lean, acidic wines, though flavoury when young.
No future. Drink up.

1968

Arguably the worst vintage since 1951; thin and acidic wines, few remain.
Avoid.

1967★

Quite attractive when young. Flowering late, July/August hot and dry followed by generally cold weather with the odd fine period. Chaptalisation enabled some attractive wines to be made. They peaked in the mid-1970s but most were cracking up by the 1980s.
Drink up.

1966★★★★

An excellent long-haul vintage. Lean rather than plump, though with good firm flesh.

Flowering was early after a mild winter and early spring. The cool and fairly dry summer was counter-balanced by a very hot, sunny September. The grapes were harvested in perfect conditions on October 6.

This is a vintage of real quality and great style; Bordeaux at its most uncompromising yet elegant. The first-growths all warrant five stars.
Drink up the lesser wines. Enjoy the top growths now and for the next 10 years.

1965

One of the four worst post-war vintages. The result of a wet summer which delayed ripening and yielded some thin, short, acidic wines.
A pity to tip the skinny but flavoury first-growths down the sink, but do not hesitate with the rest. Or keep for salad dressings.

1964★★ to ★★★★

On the whole a very good and abundant vintage, one of the biggest since the war. Now, like the wines of 1962, undeservedly forgotten.

A mild, wet winter and rather warm spring provided very good flowering conditions. The hot, dry summer resulted in a sound, healthy, ripe crop by mid-September, though the second half of the harvest was seriously affected by two weeks of continual rain, particularly in parts of the Médoc.

Latour picked early and made a magnificently beefy wine; Lafite and Mouton picked late and the wines have the thinness and piquancy of a lighter vintage. At best the wines of this vintage are agreeable, chunky, fruity and flavoury. Worth looking out for.

Many drinking extremely well, should continue to please.

1963

A poor, though not execrable vintage. Cold summer caused rot. Light, acidic wines.

Some thin but flavoury first-growths but otherwise avoid the few that remain.

1962★★★★

A vintage overshadowed by the incomparable 1961. Abundant crop, *une très bonne année*.

Cold and rainy conditions to the end of May; flowering in mid-June in good weather; very hot summer tempered by welcome showers in September which swelled the berries; and a late harvest, beginning October 9.

A firm, well-coloured vintage with some of the leanness of the '66s. Never fully appreciated.

The Pauillacs are pleasant: fullish, excellent flavour and balance; hard, dry tannic finish. Fine classic wines.

Drink now, and with considerable pleasure.

1961★★★★★

Undoubtedly the greatest post-war vintage to date and one of the best of the century. The '61s are the gold dust of the wine world. As with 1945, this was due more to luck than management.

Vegetation was advanced despite March frosts; cold weather during flowering, rain washed away pollen with the direct result of reducing the crop size. Persistent rain in July, drought in August and a very sunny September, left small, concentrated and well-nourished grapes. The pre-harvest sun brought them to full maturity, thickening the skins to a good depth of colour. The harvest began at the end of September.

The hallmarks of the '61s are intense depth of colour, concentrated bouquet, sweetness, high extract, flesh and tannin, acidity levels enabling long keeping, and also great length and aftertaste.

Some, Latour for example, are not ready, needing a further 10–20 years. Most are delicious mouthfillers now. A privilege to drink a vintage of this rare stature. Storage and provenance, however, are crucial. Some corks are deteriorating. Unmoved in a cold, slightly damp cellar is best.

1960★

Not a *vin de garde* year but some flavoury wines made. Perfect flowering weather around May 25 despite a cold January and late frosts. A good June but a cold summer followed. Latour, Palmer and Léoville-Las-Cases among the best of the '60s but all but the former now past best.
Drink up.

1959★★★★★

The Press deemed this at the time 'the vintage of the century'. Hugely popular with the English trade and certainly one of the most massively constituted wines of the post-war era.

February and March were the finest in living memory: frost at night, early morning mists and hot sun. A cold April followed and a fine summer thereafter, with much rain falling from September 13, but clearing up in time for the harvest which began on the 23rd of the month. A crop of average quantity was bought in, the results of which were rated *très grands vins*.

At best masculine and magnificent.
Despite some talk of 'lacking acidity' many '59s are still marvellous to drink, the best having the inner richness for an almost indefinite life.

1958★★

An attractive but largely ignored vintage, bypassed by the English trade which had bought '57s and then invested heavily in '59s. A cold spring but good flowering in June, the weather improved towards the end of summer; late harvest. Soft, flavoury wines.
All well past their best but can still be pleasing. Drink up.

1957★

Uneven, aggressive vintage. Perverse weather conditions: hot March, April frosts, poor flowering, the coldest August recorded. Unripe grapes picked in an early October heatwave. Despite this, popular with the trade.
Mainly raw, ungracious wines, most long past their best. Some surprises though. My advice, drink up.

1956

One of the most dismal post-war vintages. Most severe winter since 1709. Summer cold and wet.
Avoid.

1955★★★★

A good but always somewhat under-appreciated vintage. Alternating weather patterns early in the year; a fine summer with a perfect July and welcome rains in September; fine conditions for harvest on the 22nd. Optimistic reports at the time but not as attractive as the heavily bought '53s. The best, and best kept, however, are still lovely – undervalued, some warranting five stars.
The top growths, particularly of the Médoc and Graves, still perfection and will keep. All others, drink soon.

1954★

Despite one of the worst summers on record, some quite nice wines made. Rarely seen.
Drink up.

1953★★★★★

A fine vintage: the personification of claret at its most charming and elegant best.

Early, dry spring with insignificant frost; flowering started well but cold and rain caused some *couleure*; fine summer with perfect August; excessive rain in mid-September delayed harvest which eventually started October 2 in perfect weather. Average, ample yield.

A vintage that has never gone through a hard or dull period. Attractive in cask, an appealing youth, perfect maturity.

Many still in peak of perfection but best to drink soon before they fade as, like the '29s, they undoubtedly will.

1952★★ to ★★★★

Considered a *bonne année* at the time, but many wines lack vinosity and charm.

A warm spring and hot June (flowering under exceptionally good conditions); July and August were hot; September cold, picking beginning on the 17th in unfavourable weather. Below average quantity.

Pomerol and St-Emilion excelled, Graves were good, Médocs were hard and though good, firm, and long-lasting, lacked plump flesh.

Difficult to generalise for even the top growths were variable. Never as easy and delightful as the '53s though sturdy. My recommendation: drink up.

1951

One of, perhaps the worst, vintage since the early 1930s. Thin, acid, decayed.
Avoid.

1950★★

An abundant vintage – nearly double that of 1949 – of uneven quality which filled war-depleted cellars. Good flowering, but harvested in changeable weather. Middleweight, lacking the charm and balance of '49, but sometimes surprisingly nice. Rarely seen. Some good Pomerols but most successful in Margaux and Graves.
Drink up.

1949★★★★★

A great vintage following extraordinary weather conditions. After the driest January and February on record, flowering during cold and rain resulted in the worst *couleure* ever remembered; increasingly hot weather followed, with an almost unprecedented heatwave: 63°C (145°F) recorded in Médoc on July 11; storms thereafter in early September, fine harvest weather on the 27th, with a little beneficial rain.

A small quantity of supple, beautifully-balanced wines. More finesse and elegance though firmer than the '47s, less intense and concentrated than the '45s. Claret at its middle-weight, fragrant, superfine best.

Many still perfect to drink, certainly all the top St-Emilions, Pomerols, Graves and Médocs – notably Margaux and Pauillac.

1948★★★

A rough diamond, lacking polish and charm, this vintage was sandwiched between two more attractive vintages and consequently neglected.

1948 was characterised by perverse weather conditions: an exceptionally good spring then a cold summer which suffered much *coulure*, the critical month of September, however, provided good picking weather.

The crop was three-quarters the size of 1947 and although the quality was good, the '47s and '49s were – rightly – preferred.

Drink now.

1947★★★★★

Another post-war milestone, the 'Edwardian' summer produced wines of an entirely different character to the '45s: big, warm, fleshy and generous.

A late spring and fine, increasingly hot summer. Picking in almost tropical conditions began on September 19. The problematic fermentation caused by the heat resulted, for some winemakers, in 'pricking' and acidity. However, there are some rich, ripe, exciting wines. Pomerols superb.

Drink now, at their opulent best – before acidity takes over.

1946

An odd rather than 'off' vintage which suffered an invasion of locusts. Rarely seen though some, tasted recently, are surprisingly good.

Now – if you can find any.

1945★★★★★

A year which heralded a string of vintages to match, if not exceed, the quality of the 1920s and was welcome after the misery of the war. This, in my opinion, is one of the top three vintages of the century.

The crop was severely reduced by late frosts, hail, disease and exceptional drought which lasted until early into the harvest.

The wines are generally deep and concentrated and, having drawn the nutrients from the soil which would normally have fed a larger crop, are packed with flavour.

Though some are drying out, the top Pomerols and first-growth Médocs are virtually unmatched for depth of colour, richness and concentration. In my opinion a greater vintage than 1961.

1944★★

A slightly larger than average crop. Rain towards the end of the harvest resulted in wines of irregular quality: lightish, short, and

at best charming, spicy and flavoury. They were better than expected though.
Now, before they fade away.

1943★★★ to ★★★★

The best of the wartime vintages. An average sized crop after good weather conditions. Overall there was richness and fruit, pleasant but lacking persistence.
Drink now.

1942★★

After a very cold winter, a small crop of light, pleasant and useful wines. Now variable, and risky.
Drink up.

1941★★

A small crop; the vines suffered neglect and disease due to the war. More than merely interesting.
Drink up.

1940★★

Vines suffered wartime neglect. An average crop of uneven wines was produced. Some still very attractive.
Drink up.

1939★

A cold and stormy summer resulted in a large but very late vintage of light, though fragrant wines.

1938★

Bottled in the early days of the war. A below average vintage.

1937★★

An important, originally highly regarded, vintage. A dry but cool summer producing wines high in tannin and acidity. Now austere and many distinctly raw and unpleasant to drink. Margaux the best.

1936★

Bottled in 1938 after the slump. Overlooked and rarely seen, though some pleasant surprises.

1935★

An abundant vintage of irregular quality. Rarely seen.

1934★★★★

The best vintage of the decade. The grapes were saved from a two-month drought by September rain, producing a good quality, abundant harvest. Rich, now somewhat overmature, but exciting and attractive wines.

1933★★★

Light, charming wines, somewhat upstaged by those of 1934. Some still delicious.

1932

The latest harvest on record (completed December 1). Execrable wines produced.

1931

A bad summer, just saved by a beautiful autumn. Wines rarely seen but just drinkable.

1930

Bad weather, bad times, bad wines.

1929★★★★★

Considered the best vintage since 1900. A good summer followed a difficult flowering period, and an average sized crop was harvested.

The results were wines of charm and delicate balance. At this time Mouton-Rothschild was for many years the star-attraction in the salesrooms. The top wines can still be lovely despite being well past their best.

1928★★★★★

A monumental year: an extremely hot summer with some much-needed rain produced a promising harvest.

This is the longest-lived vintage of the decade. Initially overpoweringly hard and tannic, some of the top wines, Latour in particular, took 50 years to soften. The best, however, have mellowed and can still be superb.

1927

A poor year. Rarely seen.

1926★★★★

A very good year. A hard winter, cold spring and small flowering, followed by long, hot summer. The small size of the crop coincided with the 1920s boom period and resulted in prohibitively high prices.

Still incredibly rich.

1925

A sunless year, producing weak and watery wine.

1924★★★

A vintage, not unlike 1978, saved by three beautiful weeks in September following a cold spring and wet summer. Wines of considerable charm, rich but delicate, some still drinking beautifully.

1923★★

Moderate vintage; some initial charm, few wines more than faintly interesting.

1922★

Enormous crop of uneven quality. Few wines have survived.

1921★★★★

A year of exceptional heat and consequent problems of vinification. Good winemakers were rewarded with wines full of fruit, alcohol and tannin. The vintage that made Cheval-Blanc's reputation. Some still impressively good, but risky.

1920★★★★★

The first unqualified *grande année* since 1900. A mild winter, excellent spring, perfect flowering, and an exceptionally cold summer menaced by oidium and black rot which severely reduced the size of the crop to a third that of 1919. The best-kept have survived.

1910s

1919★★★ began well with a good flowering, the grapes then suffered oidium and mildew during a damp July, and were scorched by ensuing heat. Lafite enjoyed abundance whilst others were reduced by the excessive August temperatures. Moderately good, flavoury wines; though light and somewhat overtaken by acidity. **1918★★★** a good summer with no extremes of temperature. A slightly larger crop than the previous year's: good colour and sound, reasonable body; can still be quite attractive. **1917★★** was a pleasant vintage, though the quantity suffered due to a shortage of labour; now scarce, variable, mainly risky. **1916★★** produced good if somewhat hard wines, lacking charm.
  The poor summer of **1915~** saw the vines suffering from mildew, pests, lack of treatment and shortage of labour. Never tasted. **1914★★** was generally disappointing after a bright start, but some excellent wines were made: the few that survive can still be quite good. In **1913~** pests and miserable weather brought this year close to disaster. Now dried-out and tart.
  1912★★ underwent unsettled weather; an abundance of light, fairly satisfactory wines resulted; surprisingly some have survived. **1911★★★** saw a small yield of good quality wines: now variable, some still impressive; and **1910~** a small yield of insubstantial wines: thin and faded.

1900s

1909★ produced an average crop of light wines; distinctly *passé*. **1908★★** was an average year; now risky though some wines still clinging precariously to life. An abundant crop of appealing wines was produced in **1907★★** but they lacked staying power: now well past best.
  In **1906★★★** an unusually good start to the year was followed by excessive heat and drought in August which reduced the yield and produced wines of robust, high quality: now faded yet

still some remarkable survivors.

1905★★★ produced a large crop of light, moderately elegant wines; now variable, faded but flavoury. Excellent growing and harvesting conditions in **1904★★★★** produced an abundant crop, some lovely wines; amongst the great survivors.

1903~ saw a freezing April and sunless summer: poor wines; **1902★** a moderately large crop: light, ordinary wines; and **1901★** a big harvest of very uneven quality.

1900★★★★★ the start of the 20th century, was heralded by one of the finest vintages ever: excellent weather throughout the year led to a superabundant harvest; the best, and best kept, wines still beautiful to drink.

Pre 1900

1899★★★★★ was the first of the great *fin de siècle* twins: outstanding and of exquisite flavour and delicacy, the best, and most prudently stored, still beautiful to drink.

1898★★ to **★★★★** produced uneven, tannic wines which generally took time to soften; some have survived. And **1897★** was the smallest crop between 1863 and 1910 due to unusual salt winds from off the sea.

Favourable weather conditions in **1896★★★★** produced an abundant crop, and good wines: fine, delicate and distinguished; now faded. **1895** at best **★★★★** saw uneven weather conditions and picking in exceptional heat made winemaking very difficult: those saved, including Lafite who sought scientific advice, turned out remarkably well.

1894★ produced a small crop of thin, uneven wines; now faded. And in **1893★★★★** after 15 dismal years, the weather was exceptionally good, with no frosts, diseases or pests: the harvest was the earliest on record (August 15), yielding the biggest crop in 18 years of good quality grapes. Some wines are still superb, but risky.

1892★ to **★★★** saw a small crop of weather-ravaged grapes: irregular in quality; one or two survivors. **1891★** green, mediocre wines; yield severely reduced by *cochylis*. **1890★★** colour and body at the expense of quantity, which was average.

WHITE BORDEAUX

A GREAT DEAL OF WHITE WINE IS MADE IN THE vineyards of the Gironde. Most is dry and of every day quality, some is of superior quality; there are also fairly sweet wines of modest pretensions and, arguably, the greatest sweet wines of the world.

Although the climate is common to all Bordeaux districts, the weather conditions in the late autumn, after the grapes for the dry wines have been picked, are crucial for the sweet wines, and can vary significantly; moreover the methods of making the classic sweet wines are so different that they warrant separate descriptions.

Dry white Bordeaux Though a quantity of fair to middle quality wine is made in the Entre-Deux-Mers, to the southeast of Bordeaux, the finest dry whites are made from grapes, almost exclusively Sémillon and Sauvignon Blanc, grown in the vineyards scattered throughout the extensive Graves district due south of Bordeaux; the two finest, white Haut-Brion and Laville-Haut-Brion, are actually situated in the suburbs due west of the city centre.

No white wines are made in Pomerol and none to speak of in St-Emilion and its hinterlands. In the Médoc, the classic claret district, only one dry white of note is made, Pavillon Blanc de Château Margaux, though Château Lynch-Bages has recently entered this field too. White Lafite is also made occasionally, in tiny quantities for family consumption.

The white wines of the Graves share an identical climate and enjoy – or otherwise – similar variations of weather during the growing season as do the reds. For this reason, the notes on the white wine vintages will not restate in full those that appear in the preceding red Bordeaux section unless there has been some significant aberration. Differences that arise are due also to the grape varieties, their ripening dates and their specific characteristics; generally, but not always, the Sémillon and Sauvignon Blanc are picked before the red grapes, principally to capture the fresh acidity that is so essential a feature of all dry white wines.

Importantly, the majority of the dry white Bordeaux are meant to be drunk young and fresh, those made predominantly, sometimes exclusively, from the Sauvignon Blanc, within a year or so of the vintage. Only the relatively few whites made at classed-growth châteaux will benefit from bottle-age and others, made, classically, from the Sémillon and Sauvignon Blanc, should be consumed within three to five years. There are exceptions, depending on the vintage. The two great odd-men-out have already been mentioned. Both white Haut-Brion and Laville-Haut-Brion positively need bottle-age. In a top vintage these wines are too powerful to be drunk young and are both best somewhere between five and ten years after the vintage: both capable of lasting, and drinking well, for more than 20, even on occasions up to 50 years.

Sauternes A relatively small rural district of rolling hills and hamlets at the most southerly end of the Bordeaux wine region, with a fair concentration of vineyards, and 'châteaux' ranging from modest farm house to medieval castle and grand mansion.

The four communes, or parishes, plus the neighbouring

lower-lying Barsac, specialise in sweet white wine. They grow the same grapes as in Graves on their northern borders: Sémillon and Sauvignon Blanc, with a soupçon (as little as one percent) of Muscadelle occasionally added at the discretion of the proprietor.

The essential difference between these and the dry whites is that the grapes are left longer on the vines and allowed to develop a beneficial mould, *Botrytis cinerea* or *'pourriture noble'* (noble rot), the effect of which is to reduce the water content, increase the concentration of flesh and augment the sugar. *Botrytis* also adds a distinctive and highly desirable scent and flavour.

But it is a risky business. The crucial autumn weather can change for the worse or, less disastrously, lack of early morning mists will prevent or slow the formation of *Botrytis*. It is also expensive: labour costs are high, as the vineyard must be combed several times to select only the grapes at an optimum state of development; and the juice, reduced and concentrated, produces very little wine per vine.

The vintage notes that follow concern principally the classic sweet wines of Sauternes and Barsac though the same conditions apply to the lesser but similar style sweet wines of Loupiac and Sainte-Croix-du-Mont across the river Garonne to the east.

Top quality Sauternes, particularly from good vintages, not only keep well but need bottle-age to arrive at their peak of perfection. The quality, state of development and anticipated best drinking dates are summarised below.

1991

Dry white★★ Sauternes★ The vineyards of Graves and Sauternes were even worse affected by the severe April frosts than the red wine districts to the north and east. It was a wet summer, August afflicted by particularly heavy rain: 304mm (12 inches) in 1½ hours. Well-drained vineyards were least affected.

September was better, with exceptional heat on the 21st of the month, yet within a week the temperature had dropped to 10°C (50°F). The dry white harvest began on September 15 and those who picked early did best, though the crop was a fraction of normal. It then rained for 8 days prior to the vintage in Sauternes. Due to the onset of rot, both noble and ignoble, picking in Sauternes was the earliest in recent years, ending by October 17. The problem was to sort out the grey rot from noble rot. Yields were severely reduced.

Dry white: for early drinking. Sauternes, too early to judge.

1990

Dry white★★★★★ Sauternes★★★★★ An excellent year, possibly the best sweet whites of the 1988, 1989, 1990 trio. The dry whites were soft and agreeable. The winter was very mild and vines flowered very early, encouraging hopes for a similarly early harvest. Uneven temperatures prolonged flowering, however, and after May the summer was long and hot until the end of August.

Overall the dry whites have a better balance of acidity and alcohol than those of the 1989 vintage and are more exciting than those of the two preceding years. Slightly lower yields than for the reds.

A remarkable year for Sauternes and Barsac. At first the dry summer encouraged fears that there would be no *Botrytis*, but the rainfall in August and September produced perfect conditions for the noble rot and *Botrytis* appeared surprisingly early, developing exceptionally fast. Sugar levels were the highest since 1929 and vinification was therefore particularly difficult, the danger of volatile acidity being ever-present. The resulting wines, however, are superb.

Dry white: now–1995 except for the top growths. Sauternes: 1995 to beyond 2000.

1989

Dry white★★★★★ Sauternes★★★★★ The extreme heat resulted in very advanced growth. The vines flowered in May and picking in Graves began as early as the end of August. An abundant crop was harvested.

For dry wines, those winemakers who picked early, having anticipated low acidity and high sugar levels as a result of the heat, made impressive dry wines with a crisp finish. One of the most superlative ever years for the two first-growths, Haut-Brion *blanc* and Laville-Haut-Brion.

By September the heat had given way to mild, misty weather, ideal for the development of *Botrytis*. These are amongst the best Sauternes of the decade, and possibly of many previous decades. Even richer than the '88s.

Minor dry whites drinking now–1995, great Graves 1995–2010. Lesser sweet white now–1996, classed growth Sauternes 1994–beyond 2000.

1988

Dry white★★★ Sauternes★★★★★ A hot, dry summer was followed by a wet, humid and ultimately stormy September, then an Indian summer. The hot summer benefited the dry whites and those who picked before the storms produced some good wines.

The early autumn climate encouraged the spread of noble rot and provided ideal harvesting conditions for the sweet wines. Clearly an outstanding vintage for Barsac and Sauternes.

Dry white: drinking well now, the top Graves will last now to beyond 2000. Sauternes: now to beyond 2000.

1987

Dry white★★ Sauternes★ A year of uneven quality.

A cool spring resulted in an uneven flowering. The summer, though, was generally warm and dry, providing good conditions for the production of light, fresh, fruity dry white wines suitable for early drinking.

Much Sauternes production was marred by heavy storms in early October. On those estates where harvest took place before the storms, grapes affected by *Botrytis* produced some quite good quality wines. But overall not a good sweet wine vintage.

Dry and sweet both for drinking now.

1986

Dry white★★★★ Sauternes★★★★ An attractive and abundant year for dry white Bordeaux and another classic year for

Sauternes. A good spring and a very successful flowering were followed by a perfect summer. Heavy rains from mid-September, then humid, misty weather conditions, unsuitable for high quality dry whites, better for the development of *Botrytis*. The grapes were too diluted to make quality dry white wine at Haut-Brion.

The Sauternes harvest took place in drier weather and a substantial quantity of grapes was brought in before the rains returned on October 19. The best of the sweet whites need bottle-age.

Dry white: drink now. Sauternes: now–2000.

1985

Dry white*** to ******* Sauternes***** After a very harsh winter the weather improved and was fine and dry throughout the spring, summer and autumn; September was one of the driest on record.

The climate, which provided such excellent conditions for the red wines, was not so kind to the whites. Many of the lesser dry whites lacked acidity and were rather clumsy, but the wines of the top châteaux are benefiting greatly from bottle-age.

In Sauternes the drought resulted in highly concentrated sugar levels but insufficient moisture to encourage the development of noble rot. However, the harvest took place in ideal conditions from October 1 and those who prolonged picking managed to make some good sweet wines.

Top dry whites drinking now–2000; the rest: drink up quickly. Sauternes: now–1995.

1984

Dry white~ Sauternes** Very erratic weather patterns throughout the early part of the year resulted in an uneven flowering. The weather was generally fine during the summer but heavy rainfall interrupted the harvest.

Some light dry whites were made for early drinking, though most were acidic and lacked grace.

The effects of Hurricane Hortense in early October were, to some extent, dissipated by two weeks of windy weather which dried out the vines. The Sauternes growers started the harvest on October 15 and managed to produce some surprisingly attractive *Botrytis*-affected wines.

Dry white: drink up. Sauternes: now–2000.

1983

Dry white**** Sauternes***** A good year for the dry whites; they are stylish wines with good levels of acidity. Excellent and abundant for Sauternes: beautifully balanced wines with tremendous concentration of fruit. Certainly the best between 1975 and 1988.

After a wet spring, conditions were hot and dry in June and July. Rain in August and early September caused anxiety among some growers, but the following period of misty mornings and fine, warm days was perfect for the development of good levels of *Botrytis* in Sauternes. The harvesting there began on September 29.

The top dry whites will develop and improve further. Sauternes: now to well into the 21st century.

1982

Dry white★★★ Sauternes★★★ A year which produced white wines of good quality, but not of the stature of the outstanding red Bordeaux.

The vines flowered and grapes ripened fully under perfect conditions, perhaps too perfect for the dry whites which, though pleasant, lacked acidity. Moreover, *Botrytis* forming in Sauternes was completely washed away by three weeks of torrential rain towards the end of September. The wines were sweet but, like the 1970 Sauternes, lack 'golden' *Botrytis*.

Dry white: except for Laville and white Haut-Brion, drink up. Sauternes: from now to the end of the century.

1981

Dry white★★ to ★★★ Sauternes★★ Ideal weather conditions made this a good year in Sauternes. A hot, dry summer produced healthy, ripe grapes; autumn rainfall then encouraged *Botrytis* development and harvesting took place between October 5 and November 13 during an Indian summer. Many attractive, elegant Sauternes: better than the '82s but by no means great.

Dry white: should all have been consumed. Sauternes: now–1996.

1980

Dry white★ Sauternes★★ An average vintage. Cold, dismal weather early in the year resulted in a poor flowering. Conditions improved with a hot, dry August, but the weather broke, September being cold and wet. The dry whites were insubstantial but the Sauternes were saved by sunny weather at the end of October/early November, some quite pleasant wines.

Drink up.

1979

Dry white★★★ Sauternes★★★ A wet winter led to a cold spring and summer, a fine June provided good flowering conditions. A slightly larger than average crop was harvested, showers prevailing throughout. For Sauternes a late harvest with *Botrytis*. Not a very exciting year, but bottle-age will improve the sweet wines.

Dry white: drink up. Sauternes: now–1995.

1978

Dry White★★★★ Sauternes★★ The long, sunny autumn which followed the cold spring and wet summer ripened the grapes and resulted in good quality wine full of alcohol and extract. Firm, long-lasting dry whites. However, due to the absence of *Botrytis*, the sweet wines lack real character.

Dry white: the minor wines should have been drunk by now but the top wines are still improving. Sauternes: drink soon.

1977

Dry white~ Sauternes~ A cold summer and the driest September on record: a small crop of poor wines.

Avoid.

1976

Dry white★★★★ Sauternes★★★★ The year of excessive heat and drought; ripe grapes were harvested in late September. The dry wines, with the exception of those from Graves, were low in acidity, needing to be drunk quickly; the sweet wines show great style and opulence but will probably be overtaken by the '75s.
Dry whites: drink up. Sauternes: now–2000.

1975

Dry white★★★★ Sauternes★★★★★ Spring frosts then a very hot, dry summer with some welcome rain in September and good harvest conditions for both dry and sweet wines. The top châteaux of the Graves made excellent wines. Perfect in Sauternes, well-constituted and firm.
The top dry whites still drinking well. The best Sauternes should keep indefinitely though all drinking well and most best now–2010.

1974

Dry white~ Sauternes★ Miserable harvest weather resulted in mediocre Graves and poor sweet wines, Barsacs best.
Drink up, if at all.

1973

Dry white★★ Sauternes★★ In common with the reds, inoffensive, unimpressive light wines. The better Sauternes quite good.
Dry white: drink up. Sauternes: at peak now but the best will keep another 5 years or so.

1972

Dry white~ Sauternes★ A dreary vintage: many Sauternes were declassified, though some not bad at all.
Dry white: avoid the few that remain. Sauternes: drink up.

1971

Dry white★★★★★ Sauternes★★★★★ The best vintage of the decade. After a late spring and slow flowering, hopes were lifted by a pleasant, sunny summer and well-nigh ideal ripening conditions. *Botrytis* on the grapes in Sauternes for the harvest which commenced early October.
Dry white: minor Graves drink up, the top wines at peak but will keep. Sauternes: perfection now but with an almost indefinite life.

1970

Dry white★★★ Sauternes★★★ These wines enjoy a good but, in my opinion, not entirely deserved reputation. Ripe grapes producing wines more generous in alcohol than acidity. In Sauternes an Indian summer further ripened the grapes but inhibited the development of *Botrytis*. The wines, though sweet, lack colour and zest.
Dry white: drink up. Sauternes: drink soon.

1969

Dry white★★ Sauternes★ to ★★★ A poor year; the damage was done during the wet spring, with poor flowering conditions. The white grapes in Graves were somewhat unripe and acidic but in Sauternes growers were saved by an Indian summer. On the whole, rather skinny, short-lived dry wines with high fixed acidity, and variable quality Sauternes.

Dry white: acidity does, however, provide zest that the '70s lacked and, though minor wines are skinny and tart, the best are well-sustained by its life-enhancing properties. Sauternes: acidity masked by the sweetness; most drinking quite well.

1968

Dry white~ Sauternes~ A miserable spring and summer: cold, wet and sunless. Sauternes wholly declassified.
Avoid.

1967

Dry white★ to ★★★ Sauternes★★★★★ After a late flowering, a hot dry summer and wet September, the grapes for the dry whites were somewhat unripe and acidic. However, in Sauternes the harvest began on September 27 in sunny conditions, resulting in well-structured wines of breeding, good proportion and with the quality of flesh that gives richness and shape. A classic Sauternes vintage.

Dry white: with one or two exceptions (La Louvière still excellent) drink up. Sauternes: perfection now but all will keep, the top two of the vintage, Yquem and Suduiraut, indefinitely.

1966

Dry white★★★ Sauternes★★★ A cool, dry summer with no real heat until September. Both dry and sweet have a lean, firm, sinewy character and fairly high acidity, the good Graves still drinking well but Sauternes, though fragrant, lack flesh.
Dry white: drink up. Sauternes, drink soon.

1965

Dry white~ Sauternes~ Appalling weather conditions; a tiny crop of rotten grapes. Thin over-acidic wines. The third poor Sauternes vintage in a row.
Avoid.

1964

Dry white~ Sauternes~ A promising year, hot summer, ripe grapes. Early picking saved the dry whites though many lacked acidity and balance. Torrential rain ruined the harvest in Sauternes.
Drink up.

1963

Dry white~ Sauternes~ An abysmal vintage. The first of three disastrous years in Sauternes: little wine made.
Avoid.

1962

Dry white★★★★ Sauternes★★★★ A fine summer with some rain and no disasters. Good, firm dry whites. A classic vintage for Sauternes. Harvest began on October 1. An abundant crop. Well-balanced, long-lasting, elegant wines.
Dry white: the best still very good if you like Graves with bottle-age. Sauternes: perfect now, will keep up to, many beyond, 2000.

1961

Dry white★★★★ Sauternes★★★ A small crop of stylish wines, but not of a comparable quality to the majestic reds. After poor flowering conditions reduced the potential size of the crop, an August drought and sunny September further pruned the yield. The Graves, picked early, have good acidity. In Sauternes the wines do not have the lusciousness of a great vintage, but nevertheless have good shape and flavour.
Dry white: drink up. Sauternes: the best at their best now. Drink soon.

1960

Dry white★ Sauternes★ A good spring, but cold, wet summer. Graves better than Sauternes.
Drink up.

1959

Dry white★★★★ Sauternes★★★★★ Good but somewhat solid Graves, lacking a little acidity. However, in Sauternes a monumental, heavyweight classic vintage. A long hot summer with some rain just before the harvest, which started in good conditions on September 21. The grapes had a high sugar content, producing rich, powerful, massively constituted wines.
Dry white: drink up. Sauternes: perfection now but will continue for many years.

1958

Dry white★ Sauternes★★ Good summer, late harvest. Of little interest now.
Drink up.

1957

Dry white★★ Sauternes★★★ A good spring, followed by perverse weather patterns – the coldest summer and hottest October on record – with variable results. The Graves very dry and acidic. Sauternes somewhat better: clean-cut wines with refreshing acidity, but lacking flesh.
Dry white: avoid. Sauternes: drink up.

1956

Dry white~ Sauternes~ Bad weather conditions at critical times, except for a brief improvement in time for picking; a poor, ill-balanced year.
Avoid.

1955

Dry white★★★★ Sauternes★★★★★ A classic combination of influences produced a great and abundant vintage for white Bordeaux: fine July, hot and dry August, well-balanced dry whites – the best of the decade. Some beneficial rain in September lead to an early harvest in Sauternes from the 21st of the month, and to a dry October. Well-nigh perfect for Sauternes.
Dry whites: well past their best; drink up. Sauternes: at their best, perfection; drink soon before they dry out.

1954

Dry white★ Sauternes~ A dismal, damp and cold summer. Watery, ill-knit wines. Graves passable, Sauternes a wash-out.
Avoid.

1953

Dry white★★★ Sauternes★★★★ An outstanding August, wet September, picking in Sauternes from 28th of the month in perfect weather. The dry wines pleasant, ripe, perhaps lacking acidity. Sauternes almost perfect, making up in finesse what they lack in weight.
Dry whites: all over-mature by now; drink up. Sauternes: drinking beautifully; most at peak, the best will keep.

1952

Dry white★★★ Sauternes★★★ Good, firm, well-balanced dry whites. Classic Graves. Barsac more successful than Sauternes: particularly attractive, rich, crisp wines. Hail completely destroyed the crop at Yquem.
Dry wine: austere; drink up. Sauternes: drink up.

1951

Dry white~ Sauternes~ An atrocious vintage, rightly avoided by the trade.
Happily few, if any, to be found.

1950

Dry white★★ Sauternes★★★ A better year for whites than reds. In Sauternes the harvest started in damp weather but developed into an Indian summer which ripened the grapes. Some very good sweet wines.
Dry white: well past best. Sauternes: some extremely good wines showing few signs of fatigue; nevertheless, drink soon.

1949

Dry white★★★★ Sauternes★★★★★ A classic vintage with breeding and style, less abundant than 1947 and less concentrated than 1945. In Sauternes harvest began on September 27 and continued into the driest October on record. Good *Botrytis*.
Dry white: the top Graves still remaining good though deepening in colour, with ripe honeyed bouquet. Sauternes: if well kept, superb. At their peak, probably best to drink soon before they dry a little.

1948

Dry white★★★ Sauternes★★ A good though never popular year, rarely seen now. Sauternes not bad but on the lean side.
Drink up.

1947

Dry white★★★★ Sauternes★★★★★ Despite the hot summer a good Graves vintage. A great year too for Sauternes, the harvest beginning early on September 15 in intense heat.
Dry white: a few top wines, notably Laville-Haut-Brion, drinking well though untypically rich and honeyed. Sauternes: superb; rich wines at peak.

1946

Dry white★ Sauternes★ A poor summer with wines to match. Sauternes saved at the last minute by an extremely hot October. Few shipped. Rarely seen.
Hardly an option: neither dry nor sweet exist now.

1945

Dry white★★★★★ Sauternes★★★★★ The potential crop severely reduced by spring frosts. Hail, then a drought summer. An early harvest, beginning on September 10, produced small, ripe, concentrated grapes. A first-class classic vintage.
Dry white: firm, dry, well-constituted; very scarce, can still be excellent. Sauternes: rare, firm and refined; perfection still.

1944

Dry white★★ Sauternes★★★★ Despite high hopes, a light and uneven vintage. Some very good Sauternes.
Dry white: no longer exist. Sauternes: surprisingly good though rarely seen; drink up.

1943

Dry white★★★★★ Sauternes★★★★ A rich, vigorous, well-bred year. Sauternes now drying out a little.
Dry white: now deep in colour and tired. Sauternes: the best still drinking well.

1942

Dry white~ Sauternes~ Very rich, long-lasting wines with finesse and bouquet. Yquem was a great surprise.
Many dry whites still good. Sauternes still delightful.

1941

Dry white★★ Sauternes~ Lean acidic wines.
Drink up.

1940

Dry white★★★ Sauternes★ A rarely seen, indifferent wartime vintage.
Drink up.

1939

Dry white★★ **Sauternes**★★★ Quite a good year generally.
Drink up.

1938

Dry white★★ **Sauternes**★★ A mediocre year which suffered wartime neglect.
Rarely seen.

1937

Dry white★★★★★ **Sauternes**★★★★★ The high acidity, which spoiled the reds, produced long-lasting, crisp, dry whites. A classic year for Sauternes.
The best are still superb.

1936

Dry white★★ **Sauternes**★★ A mediocre, uneven year.
Rarely seen. Drink up.

1935

Dry white★★★ **Sauternes**★★ A reasonably good vintage. The wines were bottled just before the war and have rarely been seen since.
Both better dry white and Sauternes can still be good.

1934

Dry white★★★★ **Sauternes**★★★★ The second-best wine of the decade after '37. The dry wines now well past best though interesting. The sweet wines delicious.

1933

Dry white★★★ **Sauternes**★ Not a great year for Sauternes.
Good Graves can surprise.

1932

Dry white~ **Sauternes**~ A disastrous year.

1931

Dry white~ **Sauternes**~ A poor year and worse market. But Yquem quite good.

1930

Dry white~ **Sauternes**~ A disastrous year.

1929

Dry white★★★★ **Sauternes**★★★★★ A consistently good, luscious year; the best Sauternes since 1921. A particularly great vintage for Climens. Superb wines.
Some dry whites still very good; Sauternes still riding high.

1928

Dry white★★★★★ Sauternes★★★★ Firm, distinguished wines which held well. Arguably, the best vintage of the century for the dry whites. Sauternes totally different in style. Crisper, paler and less luscious than the '29s but with better acidity.
Sauternes holding well.

1927

Dry white~ Sauternes★★★ The terrible reds and dry whites of this year tarnished the reputation of the Sauternes, which had benefited from the late autumn sun. Rarely seen.
The Sauternes can still be very good.

1926

Dry white★★★★ Sauternes★★★★ A very good vintage.
Now drying out.

1920–25 SAUTERNES

1925★★ was a mediocre year: now variable. **1924★★★** a ripe attractive vintage, which can still be very good. **1923★★★** was a moderate, pleasant year, now drying out; and **1922★** saw a fairly early harvest of abundant grapes and wines which were light, but lacking quality (drink up). **1921★★★★★** underwent an exceptionally hot summer and produced outstanding whites in all the European wine districts; arguably the greatest ever year for Yquem: deep-coloured, massively constituted wine, if well kept still superb. **1920★★★** was also a good vintage, though overshadowed by the '21s: variable, some still drinking well.

1910s SAUTERNES

1919★★ variable; drink up. **1918★★** a fairly good year, the wines were firmer than those of the previous vintage. **1917★★★** softer and riper than 1916, but not for long-keeping. **1916★★★** this was a good but tough vintage, now rarely seen. **1915★★** a moderate year, little seen. **1914★★★** surprisingly good still, though some drying out. **1913★★** drying out. **1911★★★** at best fading but sound. **1910~** no reputation and rarely seen.

1900s SAUTERNES

1909★★★★ a wonderful vintage; still drinking well if in top condition. **1906★★★★** a classic Sauternes vintage; can still be superb. **1904★★★★** a great vintage; powerful wines which can still be delicious. **1901–1903~** not very good and rarely seen. **1900★★★★** a classic vintage; still rich, powerful wines.

Pre **1900 SAUTERNES**

1899★★★★ not quite as sturdy as the 1900, now variable. **1896★★★★** an excellent vintage, at its best – as Yquem can be – superb. **1895–1894~** undistinguished. **1893★★★** an extremely hot summer; heavyweight wines, can still be very good.

BURGUNDY

BURGUNDY'S HEART, THE COTE D'OR, OCCUPIES THE lower slopes of an escarpment facing southeast across the broad valley of the Saône. A relatively small strip of vineyards, its soil, vinestocks and climate differ completely from those of its major 'competitor' Bordeaux. Of the quality factors and influences here, what the Burgundians call '*climat*' is crucial, embracing soil, subsoil, aspect, drainage and microclimate. Because of multi-ownerships of vineyards the individual winemaker's approach and ability is also of fundamental importance. But above all, as elsewhere, the weather is the great dictator.

Burgundy is particularly susceptible to spring frosts and severe summer hailstorms which, though localised, can damage the grapes and taint the wine; at worst, stripping the vines of their leaves, grapes and branches. Otherwise the usual weather variations occur throughout the growing season, producing distinctive patterns of character and quality.

Red Burgundy The Côte de Nuits, at the top end of the Côte d'Or, is the most northerly of the great French classic red wine districts, producing at its best, well-coloured, well-structured wines capable of long life. Those of the Côte de Beaune are perhaps looser knit, broader – some, like the Volnays, with a certain delicacy. Continuing further to the south the red wines of Mâconnais are modest and for quick drinking, whilst those of Beaujolais have a character and life all of their own: mainly due to the Gamay grape, partly to the different soils of this hillier area, the most southerly of which being not far distant from Lyon and the start of the Rhône Valley vineyards. Although most beaujolais is produced to be quaffed young, within a year, even within months of the vintage, in years like 1989 those made in the old-fashioned way have remarkable depth and staying power.

The classic red burgundy, however, is made exclusively from the Pinot Noir grape and achieves its apotheosis in the famous village districts of the Côte d'Or.

White Burgundy Arguably the most successful, the most admired dry whites of the world. Demand exceeding supply, their price tends to be high. Nevertheless, made from the Chardonnay, the best white burgundies provide the yardstick against which the wines made from this now ubiquitous grape are matched.

Again, the heart of white burgundy is the Côte d'Or, this time the Côte de Beaune, its Meursault, the Pulignys and the great Montrachet vineyard producing archetypal wines. After that, Chablis, well to the north, halfway to Paris, with its classic, steely, bone dry whites – though in recent years more fruity, more oaky wines are emerging. And to the south, the white Mâconnais and Chalonnais which are light, dry and usually good value: Montagnys, Rully, and the Pouillys, of which Fuissé is the best known.

All but the top Côte de Beaune whites should be consumed within one to four years after the vintage. Good Meursault and Puligny-Montrachet from, say, three to six years, the bigger whites like Corton-Charlemagne and Bâtard-Montrachet from five to 12 years, and the scarce Le Montrachet, from a good vintage, up to 20 years.

1991

Just about anything deleterious that can occur during the growing season did occur: April in the Côte d'Or was warm, with early bud-burst. May was colder with frost hindering development. In Chablis, the owners of the top vineyards managed to take effective action but the lesser vineyards were quite badly frost bitten, the yield being reduced to roughly a third of normal.

Cold weather continued in June, retarding flowering, and both *coulure* and *millerandage* further reduced the crop. There were also localised hailstorms. Thereafter the summer was hot and dry though a severe hailstorm on August 22 cut a swathe through vineyards at the northern end of the Côte de Nuits. Then, in late September, 51mm (two inches) of rain fell on the nicely matured grapes, just before picking was due to commence. After this delay the harvest got underway, but a week later there was more heavy rain causing some dilution and rot problems. Those who managed to time their picking right picked healthy, ripe grapes which had the added advantage of concentration due to the reduced crop size.

In the Côte Chalonnais the harvest was small and irregular. Beaujolais appears to be the brightest spot: more southerly, less susceptible to frosts, and in 1991 enjoying one of the hottest summers this century, even hotter than the great 1947.

Red★★ Overshadowed by the 1990s and variable in quality. Atypical beaujolais: deep coloured, rich, well-structured and will benefit from bottle-age.

White★ Also variable.

Reds: likely to be suitable for early drinking – each in its class. Whites: for early drinking; by 1984 for the lesser wines, by 1986 for the premiers *and* grands crus.

1990

Yet another successful year for Burgundy. Climatically similar to the previous year, yet many growers feel that this may rank alongside the very best vintages of the 1980s decade.

The winter was unusually warm in all regions of Burgundy; February and March saw temperatures as high as 24°C (75.2°F) in the Mâconnais, encouraging very early bud-break. April and June, however, cooled down with wet, cold nights everywhere and frost in the Chablis area. Flowering was therefore later than usual, finishing in late June in Chablis, the potentially huge crop being reduced by *coulure* and *millerandage*. The summer was hot and near-drought conditions led to irregular *veraison* and shrivelling of grapes, particularly in the Mâconnais.

Picking was early, beginning on September 17 in the Côte d'Or. Yields were up on 1989 and the grapes were generally small and healthy with thick skins. September was cooler than normal, making fermentation easier and allowing winemakers to extract excess tannins.

Red★★★★★ The Côte d'Or reds are deep-coloured and concentrated with fine tannins. The Pinot Noirs and Gamays have many of the characteristics, including the ripe, raspberry flavour, of the '89s, but also have superior extract and tannin.

In Beaujolais there were rich, ripe wines, perhaps lacking fruit; not quite as good as the '89s.

White★★★★ Growers throughout Burgundy were optimistic that this was a promising year. A surprisingly large crop of rich, elegant, well-balanced wines for relatively early drinking.

Beaujolais now, most reds now–1995, grand crus 1996–2005. Minor whites drinking now, top white burgundies 1995 to well beyond 2000.

1989

The fifth consecutive successful year in Burgundy when the vineyards basked in the gloriously hot summer that all of France experienced.

A mild winter was followed by an early spring in which growth was a fortnight ahead of normal. The long, hot summer resulted in an early harvest; exceptionally healthy, ripe, grapes were picked from September 13 in ideal conditions.

Red★★★★ The harvest brought in a larger crop of red than white grapes. The Pinot Noir ripened well and produced high natural levels of alcohol. A very good year for Beaujolais.

White★★★ The Chardonnay, like the Pinot Noir, ripened well, producing high natural levels of alcohol. This is undoubtedly a good year, although there were some contrasting views among growers about the real status of the vintage. Chablis and Mâconnais best drunk young, the top wines have plenty of life ahead.

Minor generic beaujolais should have been drunk though unblended single-vineyard beaujolais excellent now and will keep – say to 1995. Lesser Côte d' Or reds lovely now–1995, top growths of good estates 1994–2005. The best whites now–1998.

1988

A very good year throughout Burgundy. For red wines this was the best vintage of the decade.

The year got off to a poor start with a mild winter and long, wet spring. Despite this, however, bud-break was early and flowering and fruit set were problem free. Almost three months of dry, sunny weather followed, culminating in an excellent, slightly larger than average harvest which started on September 26 for the red grapes and on October 4 for the whites of the Côte de Beaune.

Red★★★★★ These are deeply coloured, rich wines, combining a good balance of fruit, acidity and tannin. Although attractive when young, they also have the capacity to age well. The Beaujolais vintage also produced wines of real quality, worth laying down.

White★★★ Ripe, fresh, well-balanced wines. However, yields were high and some wines lack concentration as a result.

Beaujolais, Mâconnais and minor reds from the Côte d' Or: drink now. The best single-estate beaujolais drinking well but will keep, say, 1994–98. Retain the top reds, particularly of the leading estates, for drinking from, say, 1996–2020, the very best even beyond then. Minor whites drink now, better quality white burgundies up to about 1998.

1987

This was quite a small vintage; its reputation is improving as it matures, particularly for the reds.

A cool, unsettled summer resulted in a poor flowering and fruit set, prompting caution among winegrowers. A particularly beneficial period of unusually hot September weather followed, and picking began on October 5 in good conditions.

Red★★★★ The small yield of grapes had a high ratio of skin to juice, resulting in fairly concentrated, well-structured red wines for early to mid-term drinking.

White★★★ This was a slightly less satisfactory year for the white wines. They were firm and clean cut, but perhaps a little on the mean side.

Lesser reds: drink up. The best: now–1998. Most white should be drunk soon, the best from now–1997.

1986

A very large crop of good wines. A cold winter was followed by a mild spring; flowering took place successfully during a hot, sunny June. Excellent conditions continued through the summer with the exception of some late August and September storms, encouraging rot. The harvest began on September 29 in good weather; those who picked late made the best wines.

Red★★★★ The size of the crop had prompted concern as to its quality. Fortunately, this was largely unfounded; and where the grapes were not too swollen by the storms, the quality was good, though the resulting wines lacked the charm of the '85s being rather tough and tannic. The best appear to come from the Côte de Nuits. Worth cellaring.

White★★★★★ The whites superb: dense and concentrated, with excellent structure; definitely worth laying down. Excellent Pulignys; increasing use of oak *barriques* becoming noticeable in Chablis.

Reds drinking now–1998, save for the grands crus which should develop beyond 2000. Most good whites drinking well now but the grands crus 1995–2000.

1985

A phenomenally cold winter, during which the temperature fell as low as −25°C (−13°F) around the lower-lying vineyards of the Côte de Nuits in January, causing much damage. Nevertheless this was a consistently good year, partly because only the healthiest vines had survived the winter.

Spring was cool, resulting in a late and often difficult flowering. However, between then and the harvest the weather was fine and warm, becoming glorious in September and October. Picking began on September 26 and a larger than average crop of healthy grapes was brought in.

Red★★★★★ Rich, ripe, clean and fruity wines. Probably the best-balanced vintage since 1978.

White★★★★ Delightful wines which will last. A late harvest of healthy grapes in the Côte de Beaune.

Attractive reds, many drinking perfectly now though the best will not reach their plateau of maturity until the mid-1990s and will keep well beyond 2000. Drink the whites now except for the top growths which will be delicious until the late 1990s.

1984

By no means a great year for burgundy, largely due to the difficult weather conditions throughout the growing season.

Spring arrived late, delaying flowering until early July. A two-month drought thereafter was followed by one of the worst Septembers on record with ceaseless rain continuing into early

October. Unripe grapes were harvested, the only consolation was that the cool weather prevented the spread of rot.

Red★ This vintage was low in natural alcohol and acidity, prompting widespread chaptalisation which produced unbalanced but not unpleasant wines.

White★ The whites make light but elegant drinking; unlikely to improve.

Reds: avoid. Whites: drink up.

1983

An extremely uneven year, even by Burgundian standards, yet the reds can be outstanding.

A successful flowering followed a poor, wet spring. The summer was generally hot with the occasional period of rain and even hail in some areas. The grapes ripened well but frequently suffered from rot. Picking began on September 29, yielding a fairly small crop, particularly around the Côte de Nuits where severe hail storms had done considerable damage.

Red★★ to ★★★★ May hailstorms in and around Chambolle-Musigny and Vosne-Romanée destroyed nearly one-third of the crop, though generally the flowering was successful. A remarkable year; rot and hard tannins were the only problems, and the wines that outlive the latter will be drinking well in the 21st century.

White★★★★ Very variable but exciting wines of character and quality. The best growths from the Côte de Beaune will keep. The lesser wines were at their best when young.

Reds of the best domaines need more bottle-ageing and, all being well, should continue to develop beyond 2000. The minor whites should have been drunk but the best growths will keep and evolve well between now and the late 1990s.

1982

A mild winter was followed by a warm, early spring and correspondingly early flowering. The summer was generally fine; September and October were both hot and sunny and the harvest started on September 20.

Many growers found their cellars too small to house their bumper Pinot Noir crop and also encountered the inevitable problems of quality associated with large quantity.

Red★★ to ★★★ The excessive production of the red wines resulted in a lack of concentration. They are, however, healthy wines with ripe fruit, suitable for early drinking.

White★★ to ★★★★ Both very good and very poor wines, most at their peak during the mid- to late 1980s. The top *crus* are worth keeping.

Most reds should be consumed by the mid-1990s though some of the leading whites will be enjoyable until the end of the decade.

1981

Dismal weather during almost all the year produced a very small crop of mostly poor wines.

A cold winter ran into a warm spring, but frost attacked the vines once budding was underway and in Chablis this resulted in the loss of one-third of the crop. Miserable conditions did not relent until August during which there was some sunshine, but the harvest – September 24 until October 5 – was continually interrupted by rain. Those who picked late, however, benefited from an improvement in the weather.

Red★★ With the odd surprise, this was a very poor year for red burgundy. The best wines were made from reduced crops of highly concentrated grapes.

White★ Mediocre. Frosts in the Yonne reduced the Chablis crop considerably.

The best reds will be enjoyable for another two or three years though most would be better consumed sooner. Whites: drink up.

1980

A year of mixed results, but on the whole this was a good vintage for red burgundy.

Bud-break was delayed by a cold winter and cool spring. A cold June lead to extended and uneven flowering, though August and September temperatures were above average. Some rain fell before the harvest which ran from October 10 onwards. Those growers who picked latest produced the best wines.

Red★★ to ★★★ These were, as a result of the small crop, deep, fairly concentrated wines, especially in the Côte de Nuits.

White★★ A disappointing and uneven crop. The lack of sunshine, particularly in Chablis, resulted in acidic, austere, unbalanced wines.

The minor reds and all the whites should have been consumed by now. Some of the leading reds are drinking well but best before 1995.

1979

An abundant vintage of mainly good-quality wines. Vegetation was delayed by a cold winter and spring, then frosts during early May coincided with budding. The summer was fair with the exception of several hailstorms, one of which caused particular damage between Nuits-Saint-Georges and Chambolle-Musigny. However, the surviving grapes were healthy and a satisfactory harvest was brought in at the end of September.

Red★★★ Overall, quite good wines.

White★★★★ These too were attractive wines with a more obvious, easy charm than the harder, firmer '78s. The '78s will, however, outlast them. Very good in the Côte de Beaune.

The best reds still have a lot of life though most should be drunk before 1996. The best whites are still very good and will develop further with bottle-age.

1978

An excellent year. The small crop of good quality wines came onto the market at a time of high demand, which encouraged growers to open prices 100% above those of the atrocious '77s.

Vegetation and flowering were delayed by an unusually cold spring and early summer; the weather turned on August 20 when the grapes were setting and an excellent autumn saved the vintage. The harvest (around October 11) produced richly-coloured, alcoholic wines.

Red★★★★★ These are well-structured wines; their strength is derived from ripe grapes with a good balance of fruit, tannin, alcohol and acidity.

White★★★★★ The best year since 1971. All areas, even the minor districts, produced wines of high quality. Very firm, well-built, alcoholic wines, with fruit, extract and acidity.

A highly satisfactory vintage for reds, most of which are drinking well now, but the best will 'flower' between 1995 and 2010. Top quality whites are superb, with a maturity span beyond 2000; most though are delicious now and best drunk before the mid-1990s.

1977

Despite an ideal spring and perfect flowering, torrential rain throughout the summer, with a two-week break in August, and then severe storms later in the month, brought this vintage near to disaster. September was mercifully fine and the harvest started on October 4.

Red~ An abundant crop. Sandwiched between two far superior years the '77s attracted little attention, though considering the conditions some drinkable wines were made.

White★ These were generally better than the reds. The small crop provoked much interest from the trade where stocks were low, consequently prices were higher than really deserved.

Red: avoid. White: Drink up.

1976

1976 had everything going for it: a mild, frostless winter followed by a summer of intense heat and drought. This relented slightly in time for an early September harvest.

Red ★★★(★)? A very welcome vintage, coming at the end of the recession and following three poor quality years. These were wines with colour, fruit, extract and alcohol, but with an excess of tannin which might never ameliorate.

1976 is also notable as a good year for beaujolais; possibly comparable with the best '47s, '59s, and '64s.

White★★★★ The excessive heat ripened the grapes very early and, in order to avoid loss of acidity and an excess of sugar, the harvest was bought forward (to September 15 in Chablis). Some grapes were gathered before quite ready. The result: variable wines, some lacking life, others too hard.

Most reds can and probably should be drunk now. However, some are still very noticeably tannic, though, despite the risk of drying out, the best are worth keeping. The whites should mostly be drunk now though the firmest and best will continue to develop through the 1990s.

1975

A disastrous vintage: the worst since 1968, though marginally better for the whites. After a fine late spring and early summer the weather was generally unpleasant and grapes suffered widespread rot. A small quantity of thin, mouldy wines coincided with worldwide recession. A year which Burgundians prefer to forget.

Drink up.

1974

A mild but occasionally frosty spring, a difficult flowering and sunny summer were followed by the coldest September for many years. Picking started September 21 in cold, wet and windy weather.

Red★ Mainly dismal.

White★ Some interesting wines made, though of little interest now.

Drink up.

1973

A good start, successful flowering and a dry prelude to the summer – the driest since 1945 – which broke in mid-July with heavy rain, particularly on the Côtes.

Red★ Light, watery and unimportant wines. A late, wet and extended harvest ran from September 22 until October 18. This was a miserable year: the size of the crop ran over the permitted yield per acre and coincided with a drop in demand.

White★★ to ★★★★ Overall a good vintage for whites, comparable with, possibly better than, 1970, but the wines not as firm as the '69s or '71s. Wines of charm and fragrance but consequently at their best young. A tendency to be over acidic.

Reds: drink up. Whites: the best are still good; finish off the others.

1972

A severe winter was followed by warm weather at the end of March and the vines budded in April; summer was oddly cold but dry, and September mercifully sunny. A huge crop was picked late under good, if cold, conditions.

Red★★★ Despite being unpopular with the English (due partly to being overshadowed by the three previous years, and partly to the association with the poor 1972 red Bordeaux) these were reasonably well-structured, pleasant and interesting wines, though with a slight touch of bitterness. They are now losing their appeal.

White★★ A mediocre vintage. Some of the grapes were harvested too early resulting in over-acid wines. Others were light and lacked finesse. Nevertheless, there were many pleasant results, including some good Meursaults and Montrachets. Of little current interest.

The reds are for drinking now; only the very best are worth keeping. Drink up the whites.

1971

An outstanding vintage throughout Burgundy: vigorous, well-constituted wines.

Apart from a slightly problematic flowering, the summer was settled. August saw some hail and a poor final week but conditions picked up with a beautiful first half of September. A small but well-nourished crop of grapes was picked from September 16 onwards. In the Côte de Beaune, the area worst affected by the hail, the quantities amounted to a mere fraction of the 1970 harvest.

Red★★★★★ An impressive vintage, regarded as untypical by Burgundians. The severe pruning caused by the harsh weather resulted in unusually substantial wines. Overall, big, rich and well-structured. Many were outstanding.

White★★★★★ One of the loveliest white burgundy vintages of the period. Dry, firm, well-balanced and subtle; the Chablis,

Meursaults and Montrachets were particularly successful.

Reds are drinking well now, the best will keep beyond 2000.
The whites should be drunk now though the firmest will be
superb for another 5 or 10 years.

1970

April and May suffered bad weather but thereafter conditions
were generally fine through to October. A large crop of ripe
grapes was picked at the end of September.

Red★★ Disappointing. Pale wines, probably due to over-
production, many reaching maturity within five years.

White★ to **★★★** An uneven vintage which ranged from bad,
somewhat dull, to good. The wines were often too soft, overripe
and lacking in acidity. Most were speedily consumed.

Reds: fully mature now, drink up. Whites: drink up.

1969

After a mild winter and cold, wet spring, the grapes budded late
and were ripened by a fine, sunny summer. September was wet,
but sound, ripe grapes were gathered from October 5 onwards in
exceptionally fine conditions.

Red★★★★★ A superb vintage, not unlike 1949, but still
somewhat underrated, 1969 being tainted by Bordeaux' poor
reputation. The wines appeared to fall into two categories: light
wines for quick drinking, and a higher class which had the body,
tannin and acidity for long keeping – the first year of such
quality since 1966. This is a vintage that constantly surprises
and delights.

White★★★★★ A distinctly agreeable vintage. Firm, dry,
well-balanced classic wines, the best of which took a full ten
years to develop.

The best reds are excellent now and will keep, some
comfortably into the 21st century. Whites: drink all but the very
best now.

1968

A very poor year. Such a catastrophic vintage that the Hospices
de Beaune auction was cancelled. Some skilful winemakers who
chaptalised their white wines did, however, manage to produce
a few surprises.

Mostly long consumed, few now seen. Avoid.

1967

Favourable weather conditions, including a particularly sunny
July and August, persuaded some vineyard owners to dispense
with dusting the vines to protect them from disease. Ten days of
rain in September produced some disastrous results. Many
winemakers attempted to speed up fermentation. The wines
produced were very uneven, some particularly high in alcohol.

Red★★ Variable, but the best, especially from the *grands*
crus climats on the slopes, were delightful.

White★★★★ A better year for the whites: highly attractive,
dry, refreshing wines with good flavour. Mostly past their best
but still some surprises around. Despite this the trade showed
more interest in the '66s.

Drink up.

1966

Crops were damaged by spring hail. The summer began poorly, but conditions gradually improved. The harvest took place from September 28 in perfect conditions, the light September rain having gently swelled the grapes.

At the outset growers were worried that the harvest would be small, but ultimately were pleasantly surprised by the good quantity coupled with good quality.

Red★★★★ Overall a firm, elegant vintage. The Côte de Nuits produced the best wines, and even the less good ones from elsewhere were attractive and lively.

White★★★★ Very high quality wines which combined austerity with fragrance, good firm flesh, and sufficient fat and acidity to give them longevity. Not surprisingly, this was a very popular year which achieved consistently high prices.

Reds: the best are perfect now, the greatest will keep.
Whites: most should have been drunk though the grands crus *are still superb and will continue to dazzle with their style and richness.*

1965

A catastrophic year: rain waterlogged the soil and an appalling storm washed away some vineyards.

1964

A justifiably popular vintage with merchants. Record prices were achieved at the annual Hospices de Beaune auction.

After the hardest, snowiest winter in 20 years, conditions finally picked up in time for a perfect June flowering, and a hot dry summer reduced the by now abundant crop. September alternated regularly between rain and sun, providing perfect pre-harvest conditions.

Red★★★★ Superb, meaty, open-knit wines.

White★★★ The grapes were high in sugar and low in acidity. A popular vintage but lacking finesse, and quick maturing.

The best reds still excellent. Whites should be drunk up.

1963

A rather dreary summer and sunny autumn produced a very large crop of mediocre wines.

Red★ A poor to fair vintage which was completely overshadowed by its two good flanking years.

White★★ A much better year for white wines although very few were bought by the trade. Rather low in acidity; some good Montrachets.

Few remain. Drink up.

1962

A very good year. A cold April preceded a summer which gradually improved and culminated in a sunny August and welcome rain in September, delaying the start of picking until October 8. Exceptional harvesting weather produced a smallish crop of ripe, healthy grapes.

Hopes were that prices would come down to a more realistic level thanks to another satisfactory year, but this was not the case as sellers found themselves greatly outnumbered by buyers and prices strengthened. In retrospect good value nevertheless.

Red★★★★ Fragrant, delicious, stylish wines. The best were slow starters but ultimately attractive, exciting and well-balanced, meriting five stars.

White★★★★★ The whites have a perfect balance of body, acidity, flesh and crispness and are still worth looking out for.

Reds are firmer than the '64s, the best still superb and with years more life if well kept. Few whites remain but a grand cru, if perfectly cellared, can be delicious.

1961

A mild winter and warm spring pushed the growth of the vines months ahead of normal. However, due to uneven weather patterns in June, the flowering took nearly three times longer than average and this, coupled with a bad summer, meant that the vintage reverted to its usual timing. Conditions for harvest were good and picking began on September 25.

Red★★★ A good, appealing, fragrant and popular vintage, though not comparable to 1961 red Bordeaux.

White★★★★ Undoubtedly a good year, the wines were enormously popular – thanks partly to the success of the reds, the small size of the crop and the dismal previous vintage.

Some of the reds still delicious but best drunk soon. Lesser whites should have been consumed by now but the great white burgundies can still be superb.

1960

Unripe grapes, poor wines.

Red~ Thin, almost all consumed early.

White~ Equally thin, very acidic whites, refreshing in the early 1960s.

Drink up.

1959

Excellent for the reds but not for the whites. Good growing conditions with a hot, dry summer and sufficient rain to swell the berries.

Red★★★★★ A magnificent vintage. From the first tastings these have always been highly flavoured, richly coloured wines with plenty of extract and tannin. The most dependable of the older vintages: the last of the great classic heavyweight reds.

White★★★ Growers experienced difficulties with vinification and the wine tended to lack acidity. The more substantial wines such as Le Montrachet and Corton-Charlemagne can still be very good.

In the northerly areas the hot weather was most beneficial and produced some interesting Chablis.

The best reds are still superb. Few whites remain; drink up.

1958

The market was already inundated with high-quality wines when this moderate vintage appeared; the English trade gave it a miss.

Red★★ Rarely seen. Now fully mature; drink up.

White★ Not difficult to avoid: none to be had.

1957

After a mild spring, an early summer with extreme heat, though temperatures relented considerably with cool, grey July afternoons.

Red★★★ A good, flavoury vintage: the acid levels lending a zesty quality to the wines. A better vintage for Burgundy than for Bordeaux.

White★★★ Disastrous May frosts in Chablis destroyed almost all the vines, including those of the top growths. Elsewhere, there were pleasant, firm, fruity wines.

Some reds have survived and can be quite flavoury. But drink up.

1956

A disastrous year, menaced by disease and pests. Rarely seen.
Avoid.

1955

After a slow, cold start to the year, the weather picked up and harvesting took place under the best conditions in 20 years.

Red★★★ The reds were sound though variable, and enjoyed a fair degree of popularity. The Côte de Nuits had depth and style but lacked length and finish; the Côte de Beaunes were light and at their best in the mid- to late 1960s.

White★★★★ A delightful vintage: elegant and beautifully balanced, sitting somewhere between the solidity of the '52s and '59s and the soft ripeness of the '53s.

Reds are fully mature; drink now. The whites are past their best; drink up.

1954

Pleasant spring, successful flowering, but wet summer. The harvest saved by a late, sunny autumn. Picking began October 7. An abundant crop of uneven quality grapes.

Red★★★ Overshadowed by the '52s and '53s, this vintage was undeservedly neglected.

White★ Unripe and a tendency to tartness. Few shipped.
Drink up.

1953

Apart from a mild April, the weather was generally wet and cold until August/September when the warm sun ripened the grapes. The harvest started on September 29 under excellent conditions.

Red★★★★ Ripe, supple, attractive wines.

White★★★★ As with the reds, these were highly popular – and with good cause. Soft, pleasant and very good value, though less firm than the '52s.

The best reds, though fading, can still be delicious. Whites need drinking up.

1952

A June drought and a hot July and August with some rain, then a cool September.

Red★★★★ A very reliable burgundy vintage, tough and concentrated as a result of the drought – a close second after '59 as the most dependable of the decade.

White★★★★ As is so often the case with burgundy, the whites were better than the reds. The best reached perfection and all enjoyed great popularity, consequently few remain.

The best reds are still firm and excellent to drink; whites though are well past their best, the few that remain can be more than interesting.

1951

With '56, one of the two worst years of the decade. Rarely seen but some surprises.

1950

A vintage menaced by hail throughout the summer, the latter half was wet.

Red★ Feeble wines.

White★★★ A far better vintage for the whites. Some excellent Montrachet, great variety in the quality of the Chablis. Among the less superior wines there was a tendency to fat and lack of length.

1949

A very wet start to the year, but worries were soon quelled by a dry summer with a little beneficial rain. Harvesting began September 27.

This vintage was highly popular amongst the buyers and was bought at exceptionally reasonable prices.

Red★★★★★ First class results. Compared to the '47s, the '49s were better balanced and closer knit, consequently they held for longer. This was burgundy at its elegant best. Wines which still can be excellent.

White★★★★ Superb, supple, well-balanced wines which lasted well. Now rarely seen and tiring.

1948

Cold, wet weather which gradually improved from mid-August.

Red★★ to **★★★** A vintage unfairly sandwiched between two superior years. Some wines of very high quality but some tired now.

White★★ Virtually bypassed by the English, despite being a moderately good year.

1947

Fantastic weather conditions throughout the year gave rise to much well-founded optimism. The usual difficulties associated with winemaking in great heat affected some areas, but those who overcame them made outstanding wines.

The '47s came onto the market at a time when the old-established British wine merchants were anxious to replenish their war-depleted cellars. Wines were bought enthusiastically, and at very reasonable prices

Red★★★★ Immediately attractive, ripe wines. More stable than their counterparts in Bordeaux.

White★★★★ A ripe, delightful, early-maturing vintage. Some excellent Chablis and Bâtard-Montrachets.
Reds are still drinking well; English-bottled wines are worth looking out for. Of the whites, the top Côte de Beaune wines can still be delicious.

1946

Quite a good growing season. An abundant crop then reduced by hail, followed by a cold rainy period. Ignored by the trade.
Red★
White★★
Few ever seen. Drink up.

1945

An impressive year. Nature's severe pruning of the crop was undoubtedly the key contributing factor. Severe frosts in spring were followed by a cyclone on June 21 which devastated the ten principal villages of the Côte de Beaune from Puligny to Corton and reduced the crop to one-sixteenth of the estimated yield. The result was a small harvest of ripe, highly concentrated grapes.
Red★★★★★ Dry, firm, substantial, deep coloured, well-constituted wines which lasted admirably. The best and best-kept can still be magnificent.
White★★★★ A small crop of excellent wines with good finish. Few shipped to England. Rarely seen.

1944

This might well have been a good year, had it not been for the dismal rain which fell continuously throughout the harvest.
Red★ Light, washed-out wines.
White~ A poor vintage. None tasted.

1943

The best war-time vintage: well-nigh perfect spring, summer and autumn. A shortage of labour, bottles and corks.
Red★★★★ Many of the wines had to be kept long in the cask, hastening decline and drying them out. Nevertheless, the wines were flavoury, well-built and ripe, and the best are still drinking well.
White★★★ The best vintage between 1937 and 1945 and those that were well looked after make fascinating drinking.

1942

After a good summer the vines around the Côte de Beaune were damaged by hail. Harvesting began the following day (September 13) but was intermittent, taking four weeks to complete.
Red★★★ Good, stylish, little-known and underrated wines.
White★★ Mediocre, light wines, not often seen.

1941

Healthy vines, but a cold autumn prevented full ripening.
Red★★ A little-seen wartime vintage; few wines remain

though the reds can still be good.
White★★ Better, crisper.wines, some still surviving.

1940

Good growing season spoiled by mildew.
Red★★ Some good wines made but few remain.
White~ All consumed during the war.

1930s

Red Burgundy A decade witnessing some excellent vintages.
1939★★ and **1938★★** were both mediocre years of little interest, few now remain; but the mid-decade produced some far more distinguished wines. **1937★★★★★** was a rich, distinctive year, reported at the time to be the best since 1929 and far better than Bordeaux; the best still magnificent. **1936★** was a poor year of little interest.

1935★★★★ was a very good, abundant year, though little was shipped to the UK due to great interest in the fine, well-constituted **1934★★★★** vintage, considered then to be the best of the decade. **1933★★★★** was another good year overshadowed by 1934. **1932~**, **1931~**, **1930~** were uniformly disastrous.

White Burgundy The 1930s, like the 1920s, produced some interesting white burgundies. **1939★** and **1938★** were, however, not among them.

Undoubtedly the greatest vintage of the decade was the **1937★★★★** though only a very limited amount of it was shipped before the war and, once hostilities had ceased, merchants were seeking younger wines.

Passing over **1936★** a minor and rarely seen vintage, the next-best years were **1935★★★** and **1934★★★★** both good to very good vintages, but now of course scarce. **1933★★★** another lovely vintage in Burgundy, was still showing well in the mid-1950s but has proved disappointing more recently.

The first three years of the decade, **1930~**, **1931~** and **1930~** were all uninteresting.

1920s

Red Burgundy Including one of the best-ever burgundy vintages, seven very good to excellent years, two mediocre and only one poor.

1929★★★★ was a classic vintage of immediate appeal, combining quantity with quality which, if well-cellared, lasted remarkably well. **1928★★★★** survived the hazards of difficult weather to produce fine, firm wines. Leaving aside the dismal **1927~** the other great year was **1926★★★★** a small vintage, the best wines of which were fabulous, though few tasted recently.

1925★ was a disappointing vintage; **1924★★★★** very attractive despite the difficult weather conditions, although not as exciting as **1923★★★★** which produced a small quantity of very good wines.

1922★ was a moderate vintage following two more very good years: **1921★★★★** and **1920★★★★** the latter despite having faced bad weather and disease.

White Burgundy A decade that included some outstanding wines. **1929★★★★** was a magnificent soft, ripe vintage, but not as crisp as the excellent, firm, nutty **1928★★★★★** which was certainly the best vintage between 1921 and 1937. If well kept the 1928 whites can still be excellent.

The four mid-decade vintages – **1927★ 1926★★ 1925★** and **1924★** – were generally uninspiring, as was the **1922★** but **1923★★★★** was also very good for white burgundy.

Even better was the remarkable **1921★★★★★** a magnificent vintage for white wines throughout France and Germany, though the few remaining white burgundies are now scarce and tiring. **1920★★★** was a good vintage.

1910s

Red Burgundy This was a decade which included three exceptional years of very high quality as well as its fair share of unexceptional years.

Favourable weather conditions leading up to an excessively hot August in **1919★★★★★** produced a small vintage of outstanding, fruity, ripe wines, which can still be good.

1918★★ 1917★ and **1916★★★** were three moderate years, the best of which was 1916. The second first-rate vintage of the decade was **1915★★★★★** which enjoyed an abundant quantity of superb quality grapes that made full, fruity wines.

Passing over the three years preceding 1915, the other great year was **1911★★★★★** a magnificent classic burgundy vintage, the perfect summer and early harvest yielding a small crop.

1900s

Red Burgundy The first decade of the 20th century included some remarkable vintages, although, inevitably, scarce now. **1909~** mediocre. **1908~** was a poor year due to unpredictable weather; **1907★★★** was a good year, producing light wines, few of which are now seen.

The best vintage was **1906★★★★★** an ideal growing season and early harvest, perfect wines, the best can still be lovely, and even better than those of **1904★★★★** the other good vintage of the decade. Again, the conditions were perfect, resulting in stylish, soft wines. **1905~**, **1903~**, **1902~**, **1901~** of no interest.

1900★★ was not as good as its counterpart in Bordeaux, but did produce an abundant yield of moderately good wines.

1900–1919

White Burgundy 1919★★★★ was one of the three great vintages of the 1910s. The other two being 1911 and 1915.

1906★★★★ was the outstanding vintage of the preceding decade. Those which were well cellared remained more than just interesting for a considerable length of time.

Pre 1900s

Red Burgundy (the best vintages): **1898★★★ 1894★★★ 1893★★★** (an interesting year which produced some extremely good wines made in conditions of great heat), **1865★★★★★** and **1864★★★★** (magnificent, can still be lovely to drink).

RHONE

LOOKING RATHER LIKE AN APPLE ON A STRING, THE narrow strip of vineyards along the banks of the Rhône eventually opens out across a broad plain. The division between the wine areas of the north and south is distinct: the microclimates differ, as do the vine varieties grown, and styles of wine produced.

Red wine The vineyards to the north are on steep slopes flanking the river. The two principal red wine districts being Côte-Rôtie, adjacent to Vienne not far south of Lyon, and Hermitage. Two lesser districts, St-Joseph and Cornas, are on the right bank of the Rhône, more or less opposite Hermitage; the vineyards of Crozes-Hermitage above and behind Tain L'Hermitage. In the key northern districts high quality, sturdy, long-lasting reds are predominantly made from one grape variety: Syrah. Vintages are important. The best repay keeping.

Châteauneuf-du-Pape is a small town just north of Avignon. Its vineyards, some of the most important of the southern Rhône region, are on a wide plateau of stoney soil upon which up to 13 permitted vine varieties are grown. It is a hot district. The grapes are literally sunburnt, the pigment extracted from their thick 'tanned' skins resulting in deeply coloured wine. The hot sun, supplemented by heat-reflecting pebbles which act like night-storage heaters, produces a naturally high sugar content which converts into a proportionally high level of alcohol. Wines of power rather than finesse result, but with richness, softness and depth of fruit.

Wines designated Côte du Rhône tend to be lighter in style, best drunk young. Even the best, like Gigondas, should be consumed within two to four years of the vintage. They are not individually commented on in the notes that follow: a good year in Châteauneuf will generally also be good in the Côtes du Rhône.

White wine The three principal districts are Condrieu, just south of Côte-Rôtie, Hermitage and Châteauneuf-du-Pape, all of these producing only relatively small quantities of dry white wine.

A tiny amount is made in Condrieu from one grape variety, Viognier. Its most famous vineyard, with its own official appellation, is Château Grillet. Most are best drunk young, within, say, three years of the vintage.

The white wines made in Hermitage, from Marsanne and Roussanne grapes, combine delicacy with sturdiness and the best keep well. White Châteauneuf-du-Pape is relatively rare, it often has a distinct touch of sweetness and, lacking high natural acidity, should be drunk relatively young.

The weather conditions in the north and south of the Rhône can be taken as the same for white as for the preceding red.

1991

Red★★ White★★★ An uneven year, both climatically and for the resultant wines. The winter was unusually cold, March was mild and wet, April and May dry but cooler than usual – though the region escaped the frost damage suffered elsewhere in France – and vegetation was delayed. Flowering was from May 25 to June 20, Grenache in the south being seriously hit by *coulure*. July and August were hot and dry, enabling the vines to catch up. However, mid-September heavy rains in the northern

Rhône dashed hopes of a top class harvest: it took place between September 20 and 25, with rainy interruptions. Some rot in Côte-Rôtie but grapes healthier than expected.

In the south the surviving Grenache grapes had ripening problems. Late summer storms and humidity in September caused some rot. A small crop of mainly light red wines in Châteauneuf, but both in the north and south white wines are reported to be good, the grapes being picked before rain set in.

Châteauneuf and the reds from the south are lighter than usual and will develop early, say 1994–97; from Hermitage and Côte-Rôtie the reds will be middle-distance runners; the whites, with good acidity, to be drunk early, 3 to 4 years after the vintage, Condrieu first then white Hermitage.

1990

Red***** White**** Drought prevailed in many areas of the Rhône but the wines were, like those of the previous year, powerful and promising, if a little less aromatic.

Throughout the north flowering was early and, where the weather turned cold, there was some *coulure*. Rain was only very localised, but the heat was less intense than in 1989 and July enjoyed some cool nights. Most growers started to pick in mid-September and the grapes were in ripe, healthy condition.

Further south there was good rainfall during May and ripening was advanced. Harvesting of whites at Châteauneuf, where the rainfall had allowed the grapes to ripen fully, began September 5 and for reds September 10.

Overall, these wines were slightly lower on acidity than those of 1989, particularly in the south, but tannins were firm and alcohol levels high, indicating that these wines will be slow to open up but full of promise and staying power.

Sturdy, long-lasting reds in north and south: Châteauneuf drinking 1995 to well beyond 2000, Hermitage 1998–2020, Côte-Rôtie even longer. Whites to be drunk earlier, now–1996.

1989

Red**** White***** This was a very mixed year in the Rhône, ranging from good to very good. The long, hot summer which produced so many good wines throughout France caused serious drought throughout the Rhône region.

Where rain did fall it was very localised. Some areas were, however, at a greater advantage than others: the older vines with longer roots were able to draw moisture from the subsoil, vines on clay-based soil benefited from clay's capacity to retain water.

The grapes harvested late produced better wines than where growers had panicked and picked early. Potentially excellent wines were made in Côte Rôtie – one of the few areas receiving some precious rain. Châteauneuf was also successful, producing rich and complete reds. Hermitage less reliable, though the best reds are rich and complex and whites are deep and flavoury. White wines from elsewhere are attractive but low in acidity.

Châteauneuf drinking 1995–2005, the best reds from the north 1998–2000. Whites now–1996.

1988

Red**** White**** A very good year along the length of the Rhône, the wines from the north being excellent.

Hail and rain around the Côte Rôtie during flowering reduced yields and concentrated the crop, and excessive humidity during the spring and early summer caused problems in the south. Thereafter, the weather was hot and dry with sufficient rain in August to swell the grapes. Early picking avoided the problems caused by later rains.

The crop was of average size and made rich wines with good levels of tannin and fruit. The white wines are generally of good quality, possibly for long keeping.

Top reds drinking 1994 to well beyond 2000. The whites of both Condrieu in the north and white Châteauneuf best now–1996, white Hermitage to the end of the century.

1987

Red★to ★ ★ ★ White~ A mixed year. In the north of the region the weather was satisfactory and good wines were made at Côte Rôtie. Hermitage was not so fortunate: rain fell during the spring and flowering, resulting in an incomplete fruit set. Stormy weather in August did not relent for the harvest (mid-October) and consequently the vintage was less than perfect.

The weather in the south was worse, with rain, storms, fog, even a mass invasion of caterpillars. Light, early-drinking wines.

Côte Rôtie now–1996. All other reds for early drinking. Whites: drink up.

1986

Red★★to ★ ★ ★ ★ White★★★ Warm, dry weather during the summer. September dull, rain at the end of the month delaying the harvest which began on October 10. Those who selected carefully avoided the problems of pests and rot resulting from the wet weather. Further south the good weather held during the vintage, which lasted for one month from October 6.

Some good, long-lasting, tannic reds from Côte Rôtie to Châteauneuf. Most drinking well now but will continue developing. Whites now mature.

1985

Red★★★★★ White★★★★ After a severe winter and cool spring, the weather improved, with good flowering in early June. The summer was hot, dry and sunny and harvest took place in good conditions from September 16 until October 11.

Outstanding reds, rich, long-lasting.

Reds from the southern Rhône drinking well now though the best Châteauneuf, in common with Hermitage and Côte Rôtie, even better between 1995 and 2010. Whites: drink now.

1984

Red★★ White★ A small crop of moderate quality wines. A late flowering took place in good weather, thereafter conditions were unsettled, becoming increasingly cool and wet. The harvest ran from September 19 to October 15.

Overall, these were not wines for keeping. However, some, mainly those made from the Syrah, are holding well.

Drink up the white and most reds, with the exception of good Hermitage and Côte Rôtie which will continue to evolve to, say, 2000.

1983

Red***** White*** Flowering took place during an unsettled June, and a magnificent hot, dry summer followed. The harvest was early, beginning on September 12 for the white grapes. *Coulure* reduced the Grenache yield to below average.

The red wines from both the north and the south are excellent. They are rich and concentrated with hard tannins which will soften with maturity.

Châteauneuf-du-Pape now mature and drinking well. Hermitage and Côte Rôtie now–2000. Whites, drink up.

1982

Red**** White**** A very large crop. As is often the case with such a big harvest the quality varied considerably, but the best were excellent.

Summer was long and very hot; heavy rains in August continued until harvest began on September 7. These conditions led to problems: the heat reduced acidity levels, fermentation was difficult; many wines seem 'cooked' as a result. Furthermore pre-harvest rain reduced the concentration of the grapes.

Growers who picked carefully, did not overcrop, and who controlled fermentation, produced the best wines. A vintage often paired with 1983: it is holding well but will not last as long.

The best reds, and there are many good ones from north and south, are drinking well and will last until the turn of the century. Whites need drinking.

1981

Red** White** Rain in the north during the flowering and the harvest seriously disrupted this vintage. Nevertheless some good wines were made, particularly those from the Côte Rôtie, which needed at least ten years to mature.

Further south, cold weather during the flowering resulted in an uneven fruit set and reduced quantities. After a summer drought the harvest began on September 14.

A moderate vintage; rich, concentrated wines from Châteauneuf-du-Pape though, which, like the better wines from the north, have improved with time.

Though laden with bitter tannins the wines of Châteauneuf have ameliorated somewhat and should be drunk soon. The wines of Hermitage are mainly fully developed, the best Côte Rôtie drinking well.

1980

Red** to *** White** In the north of the Rhône the year started badly with poor weather during the spring and flowering period. As a result not all the flowers set and the crop was small. The weather improved during the growing season and a late harvest began on October 8.

In the south the weather was generally fine throughout the vintage. The largest crop ever recorded was harvested from September 25.

Fairly good, concentrated wines which have, along with the '79s, '81s and '82s, always stood in the shadow of the great '78s. The whites were best drunk young.

Drink up.

1979

Red★★ to ★★★★ **White★★★** Favourable weather conditions produced wines of high quality. In the north temperatures were cool until late July; thereafter dry, sunny weather held for an abundant harvest beginning late September in Côte Rôtie, while around Hermitage rains delayed the harvest until October 8.

A good year for the south: after a late budding, flowering took place quickly in good conditions. Some variability in the wines can be found where the vines suffered from drought.

Overall, a moderately good vintage: wines from the north were concentrated with good levels of acidity and tannin, with good ageing potential; those from the south were fragrant and soft. Most whites were consumed during the mid-1980s.

Now fully mature. Drink soon.

1978

Red★★★★★ White★★★★★ Terrible weather conditions conspired to make this a very difficult year for growers, yet with excellent results: the best vintage since 1911.

A cool, wet spring reduced yields; flowering was late and slow and the remaining summer hot and dry (too dry for some) through to the harvest. Picking began around late September/early October.

Throughout the Rhône these were big, tannic, rich reds with the acidity for long keeping; whites should still be on top form.

Astonishing reds, packed with fruit, extract and alcohol, drinking well, the top wines from Hermitage and Côte Rôtie with a 20–40 year life span. Whites fully mature.

1977

Red★ to ★★ **White★** A poor year in the northern Rhône (due to the weather) which produced thin, acidic, unripe wines.

In the south, conditions improved, with fine weather during September and October allowing winemakers to produce attractive but lightweight wines.

Drink up.

1976

Red★★ to ★★★★ **White★★★** A hot, dry summer produced ripe, concentrated wines in the northern Rhône – very good in Cornas, Hermitage and Côte Rôtie – at worst the whites lack acidity and are variable. The south enjoyed similar weather, but high hopes were dashed by rains during the harvest in late September. Here too, good wines but not for long keeping.

The best Côte Rôtie and Hermitage at peak now. Whites all past their best.

1975

Red★ to ★★ **White~** A poor year in the north and south. In the south August rains had a disastrous effect on many of the grapes which had ripened too early, while benefiting those which were ready late. Problems were later exacerbated by a hot, dry Sirocco wind blowing in mid-September. Thin, astringent wines, lacking fruit and concentration resulted: very short-lived.

Drink up.

1974

Red★ to ★ ★ ★ **White~** The second of two large vintages throughout the Rhône. Early autumn rainfall diluted the grapes in the south. Overall, a mediocre year; the best wines coming from Hermitage and Châteauneuf where those made in the more traditional style were capable of ten years of life.
Drink up.

1973

Red★ to ★ ★ ★ **White~** Heavy rains in early September resulted in a huge crop throughout the region. The wines from the Côte Rôtie had good colour but were a little light; best being suited for early drinking. There was some hail damage in Hermitage, but the reds and whites from this region, nevertheless, had good ageing potential. Further south the wines were light and low in acidity: best drunk young.
Drink up.

1972

Red★ to ★ ★ ★ ★ **White★★★** A disappointing vintage in the Côte Rôtie where wines were acidic and hard. A better year in Cornas and Hermitage where a small crop contributed both good colour and flavour. Some attractive wines in Châteauneuf.
Fully mature. Drink up.

1971

Red★★★★ to ★ ★ ★ ★ ★ **White★★★** A very good vintage. The Côte Rôtie produced big, full-bodied wines with real ageing potential. Harmonious, attractive, lighter wines from Hermitage. Southern Rhônes also very good, though with lower levels of acidity they will not age quite as long as those from the north.
Attractive reds, now fully mature.

1970

Red★★★ to ★ ★ ★ ★ ★ **White★★★** An excellent year in the south, and very good in the north: a vintage with real ageing potential. Hot, sunny weather during the growing season. Many rich, well-balanced wines were made throughout the Rhône.
Fully mature, the best still drinking well.

THE BEST OF EARLIER VINTAGES:

Côte Rôtie 1969★★★★★ 1967★★★ 1966★★★★ 1964★★★★★ 1962★★★ 1961★★★★★ 1959★★★★★ 1957★★★★ 1955★★★★ 1953★★★★★ 1952★★★★ 1949★★★★★ 1947★★★★ 1945★★★★★

Hermitage 1969★★★★ 1967★★★★ 1966★★★★ 1964★★★★★ 1961★★★★★ 1959★★★★ 1957★★★★ 1955★★★★ 1953★★★★ 1952★★★★★ 1949★★★★★ 1947★★★★ 1945★★★★★

Châteauneuf-du-Pape 1969★★★ 1967★★★★★ 1966★★★ 1964★★★★★ 1962★★★★ 1961★★★★★ 1959★★★ 1957★★★ 1955★★★★ 1953★★★ 1952★★★★★ 1949★★★★★ 1947★★★★ 1945★★★★★

LOIRE

A RELATIVELY NORTHERN DISTRICT OF FRANCE, with a maritime climate at its western end, the well spread vineyards along the meandering banks of the Loire and its tributaries mainly produce distinctly light, dry and acidic wines, best drunk young. Most are white, some are rosé, just a few are red: Chinon, Bourgueil and Sancerre Rouge.

Vintages vary of course, some producing wine more acidic than others. Contrarily, the rare very hot summer, such as 1989, does not produce the most typical Loire wines, though the reds and the sweet wines benefit from the extra ripeness.

The dry to bone dry whites such as Muscadet, Sancerre and Pouilly-Fumé should be consumed within one to three years after the vintage, as should Anjou Rosé whose main attractions are its pink colour and freshness. They do not feature in the notes on the older vintages.

However, the semi-sweet (*demi-sec*) Vouvray and the glorious Vouvray *doux*, Coteaux du Layon, Bonnezeaux and Quarts de Chaume which, in certain years, are beneficially affected by *Botrytis*, the same 'noble rot' responsible for Sauternes, keep marvellously.

It should be emphasised that great years are few and far between; 1988, 1989 and 1990 are a trio unlikely to be repeated.

1991★

A disastrous year climatically. Of all the French regions, the worst hit by April frosts which decimated the well-advanced shoots after an enticingly mild spring. Chinon and Bourgueil were virtually wiped out. Flowering, late June, was also hampered by cold and, adding to frost losses, *coulure* and *millerandage* reduced the potential crop. A hot and dry summer raised hopes which were finally dashed by rain and rot-causing humidity at the end of September. By dint of careful selection, however, some good wines were made, albeit in small quantities.

Light and acidic, most should be drunk early. A small amount of the sweeter Quarts de Chaume for drinking 1994–96.

1990★★★★★

The drought of 1989 continued into 1990, making this a good year but, as with many areas in France, acidity levels were a little too low.

Extremely mild weather during winter and spring which, with the exception of a very hard frost in Muscadet at the beginning of April, encouraged an early flowering (mid-May), but cold weather in some areas, including Anjou, in early June meant uneven ripeness.

The desert-like heat scorched many of the grapes, especially in Vouvray, but the late summer rain then swelled them slightly. Picking began August 29 in Muscadet, September 24 in the central Loire and Sancerre, and October 8 in Vouvray.

In Muscadet the wines are better-balanced than those of the previous year, although quantity was down, while white wines from Sancerre are rich but low in acidity, making them suitable for early drinking. In Anjou the crop was larger than the preceding year's, and this is destined to be an excellent year for the sweet whites of Coteaux du Layon thanks to early morning October mists which encouraged the development of *Botrytis* on

the grapes. Also good for Vouvray.
   Muscadet, Sancerre and Vouvray sec *drinking now–1994,*
Vouvray demi-sec, doux *and Coteaux du Layon now–1999.*

1989★★★★★

An outstanding year for Loire wines; one which might well
become the vintage of the century.
   A mild winter and exceptionally hot summer encouraged
very early growth. Budding was in February and flowering three
weeks ahead of normal in perfect conditions. Picking in
Muscadet began in late August and Vouvray on September 20.
   The sun-ripened Cabernet Franc grapes in Chinon, Saumur
and Bourgueil produced beautifully rich, powerful red wines
with high natural alcohol – perfect candidates for long keeping.
   Growers from the Muscadet, Sancerre and Pouilly vineyards
produced plump, rich wines lower in acidity than normal,
making this an untypical vintage, close to '59 and '64 in style.
   Chenin Blanc in Vouvray and Anjou came into its own this
year, especially *demi-sec*. Sweet whites, with age, will be classics.
   Muscadet and Sancerre drink now. The demi-secs *from*
now–1998, the magnificent sweet wines of Vouvray and Coteaux
du Layon from 1995–2020. The reds, usually dry and over-
acidic, are well-constituted and will keep well, say 1994–2000.

1988★★★★

An abundant vintage of very good quality wines throughout the
Loire; for the sweet whites, it was an excellent year.
   A mild, wet winter developed into a warm, sunny spring,
pushing bud-break and flowering about ten days ahead of
normal. Good weather continued throughout the summer and
the harvest continued from mid-September into October for the
Cabernet grapes around Chinon and Bourgueil. These were rich,
well-balanced wines with soft tannins.
   Grapes for sweet whites thrived during the mild autumn and
developed good levels of *Botrytis*. Some growers harvested as
late as November, producing wines of 14% alcohol. Coteaux de
Layon, Quarts de Chaume and Bonnezeaux stand comparison
with the great '59s. *Demi-sec* and *moelleux* will keep.
   Dry white: drink now. Classic sweet wines: now–2005.

1987★

A very mixed vintage which does not on the whole stand
comparison with the years on either side.
   A cool, damp spring led to late and protracted flowering and
uneven fruit set. The weather improved, with plenty of sun
between July and September, but broke during the harvest,
necessitating careful selection of the grapes.
   Those who picked early and whose grapes had ripened fully
produced good wines; elsewhere grapes were picked unripe and
swollen by the September rains. This was particularly the case
for the red wines of Chinon, Bourgueil and Saumur which
produced attractive, but light, acid-deficient wines.
   The dry whites, in particular Muscadet, were the exception
this year. Picking was completed before the rains came and
good, though variable, wines for early drinking were made.
   Vouvray's *méthode champenoise bruts* worth watching for.
Drink up.

1986★★★★

After a cool, wet start to the year, the weather improved and flowering took place only one week later than normal.

Overall, this was a good year for the reds. Some good Cabernet Franc wines were produced in Chinon, Bourgueil and Saumur where there was enough sun to fully ripen the grapes.

The fine summer provided ideal growing conditions for the dry white wines. The Sauvignon grapes were fully ripened, yet maintained a good level of acidity. A good year for Sancerre, and the Pouilly-Fumé reputed to be the best of the decade.

A year of above average quality for the sweet whites from Vouvray: they were elegant wines with a flowery fragrance. Some very good Vouvray *mousseux* was made late in the year.

All at peak now though the relatively few demi-sec *and* doux *will keep a while longer.*

1985★★★★

A highly satisfactory year, particularly for the reds and the sweet whites.

After a wet spring the weather picked up and remained hot and dry right until the end of the vintage. Grapes were harvested in ideal conditions from September 30 until November 10: pickers were able to go through the vineyards several times, enabling them to harvest the grapes at their optimum ripeness.

The reds were big, ripe and attractive; well-suited for early drinking. In the districts where sweet wine is made, growers who waited were rewarded by the development of noble rot and produced some excellent Chenin Blanc wines.

The Vouvrays were soft and dry with a perfect balance of sugar and acidity; they have excellent ageing potential.

The dry whites and reds need drinking though the Botrytis-*affected sweet wines will keep longer.*

1984★

A poor vintage throughout the Loire. A wet spring developed into a poor, cloudy summer, which was followed by a wet September. The wines were on the whole harsh and acidic. As the acidity fades some of the sweeter wines may show more style but, with the exception of some good Vouvray *mousseux*, this is not a vintage to look out for.

Drink up.

1983★★

A large crop of good wines. Spring and summer were wet and humid with some August hail-storms, but conditions improved mid-October in time for the harvest. The poor start to the year produced slightly light, acidic, dry wines. The sweeter styles benefited from the good October weather; some were judged to be slightly too acidic but, for the Vouvray, this meant wines with good ageing potential.

Drink up, though demi-sec *will still be pleasing.*

1982★★★

Good weather prevailed throughout the summer but there were some violent storms during the harvest. On the whole this was

not a memorable year, although Vouvray produced some good, dry wines. Drinking well in the mid-1980s but not worth keeping.
Drink up.

1981★★

A very small, modest vintage. Late spring frost damaged the buds and consequently reduced the crop, but the weather was fine thereafter. Good, fragrant wines were made around Vouvray; they were worth keeping but are now very scarce. Some wines lacked acidity.
Drink up.

1980★★

A good spring but protracted, wet summer. The harvest in Anjou, Touraine and Vouvray took place under snow from October 11 to November 11. Some pleasant wines nevertheless.
Drink up.

1979★★★

A good year. Budding was late after a slow, wet spring, July was dry and August wet, September started warm and dry but saw some rainfall towards the end of the month. Dry, fairly well-balanced whites and light, balanced reds. Best for early drinking.
Drink up.

1978★★★ to ★★★★

A cold, damp spring caused delayed flowering and *coulure* and *millerandage*. July hail caused further damage but late summer and autumn were sunny. A small crop.

This was a vintage which developed slowly, the sweet whites revealing themselves as remarkably well built; also particularly good for Sancerre and Pouilly and the dry whites of the mid-Loire. Reds for long life.
Reds now fully mature. The few remaining whites should be drunk up.

1977

A poor year. A long, wet winter and spring with an exceptionally cold spell in April when temperatures sank to −8°C (18°F). This led to a long, laborious flowering with *coulure*, then patches of mildew during the summer. Thin, dry whites and light reds.
Few seen. Drink up.

1976★★★★

The best vintage of the decade. A cold, dry winter and early, warm spring. Flowering was also advanced; summer was very hot and very dry but temperatures cooled down in September. The harvest was, nevertheless, much ahead of normal (beginning early September).

Unusually powerful wines; Pouilly Fumé was more like burgundian Chardonnay. Reds were well-built with long life.
Reds and sweet whites fully mature. The dry whites should have been drunk by now.

1975★★★

Spring was late but warm, thereafter a very normal growing season with the harvest starting in early October. An average sized crop of good wines. Fresh supple whites which were slightly superior to the reds. The richer wines have life yet.
Sweet wines still drinking well.

1974★

A large crop, after normal growing season, produced mediocre wines: the best reds and whites had quite good ageing potential.
Few if any remain. Drink up.

1973★★

A mild winter and spring encouraged a large crop, but cold wet weather in July, with occasional hail, caused some damage. Mediocre wines, although a good year for Sancerre and some well-structured reds.
All consumed by now.

1972

A cold year. Spring frosts and rain persisted well into the summer; picking was late as a result. The crop was of average size. Mediocre wines, some good whites and light reds but on the whole a year to forget.
Avoid.

1971★★★

A warm but short spring was followed by a stormy summer with very damaging hailstorms. A small crop of well-balanced wines for keeping. Acidic.
Some good Vouvrays and Coteaux du Layons still drinking well. All others passé.

1970★★

A long, wet spring resulted in an abundant flowering. A stormy summer followed and harvest produced an abundant, pleasant crop. Soft, well-balanced wines. Not a year for dessert wines.
Avoid.

OTHER GOOD/GREAT VINTAGES

1964★★★★★ produced great sweet wines, still on top form; and **1959★★★★★** magnificent Vouvray, Coteaux du Layon, and outstanding Moulin Touchais.

Excellent dessert wines were made in **1949★★★★** (at their peak now) and in **1947★★★★★** the greatest vintage for classic Coteaux du Layon, Quarts du Chaume and Vouvray *doux* – still marvellously rich. **1945★★★★** also produced very good, firm, sweet wines.

1937★★★★★ was the best vintage of the 1930s: wines with excellent acidity. **1934★★★★** was very good too, though tiring now. And **1928★★★★★** another great vintage: the best sweet wines still beautiful to drink.

ALSACE

WITH THE EXCEPTION OF SMALL QUANTITIES OF RED wine and even rarer rosé, virtually all the wines of Alsace are white, the vast majority made to be consumed whilst they are young and fresh.

The dry whites made from Sylvaner and Pinot Blanc, and the less often exported Zwicker blend, should be drunk between one to three years after the vintage. However, when it comes to the major grape varieties, Riesling, Gewurztraminer and the too-little known Tokay Pinot Gris, vintages are important, those of the highest quality achieving sublime heights and capable of remarkable longevity.

1991★

After three years of drought the rains came, but not at the most propitious moment. Happily Alsace's vineyards did not suffer from the frosts that crippled other districts and the flowering took place in good weather conditions. However, due to lack of moisture in the soil, the grapes were small. Hail in August devastated some vineyards and heavy rain hindered development. More rain in September delayed the start of picking until early October and the protracted harvest ended a month later. A small crop of moderate and variable quality.

All but the grands crus and the relatively few late-harvested wines are for drinking soon.

1990★★★★★

The second of two excellent vintages, very similar in style to 1989, but smaller in quantity. Particularly good for the sweet dessert wines.

Alsace had no real winter, no frost or snow, and the vines began to grow three weeks ahead of normal in drought conditions. Budding began in late May, but cold, wet weather followed, resulting in both *coulure* and *millerandage*, in particular affecting the more delicate Muscat, Gewurztraminer and Tokay Pinot Gris varieties.

September onwards enjoyed a mixture of rain, fog and brilliant sunny weather. The harvest began on October 4 and quantities were down by around 25% from the previous year. The grapes were beautifully healthy, but the absence of *Botrytis* meant that no Sélection des Grains Nobles wines were made. A very high sugar content and low acidity necessitated very careful winemaking. This was, however, the third successive year in which late-harvest wines were made: an exceptional vintage.

Overall, the wines are characterised by their richness and roundness, due to particularly high levels of ripeness and a smaller crop than usual, especially for Gewurztraminer and Muscat grapes. Thought by many to be comparable climatically, and possibly superior in quality, to the great 1961 vintage.

A good ripe vintage, most of the wines being enjoyable whilst young and fruity. The top quality wines made from the 'noble' grape varieties from, say, now–1998.

1989★★★★★

An admirable vintage, combining abundance and excellent quality. The late-harvest vintage was the largest ever, producing extremely powerful wines, some reaching 214 Oechsle (30% potential alcohol).

A hot, dry summer provided ideal growing conditions, pushing the growth well ahead of normal. Some areas suffered from drought but early September saw some relief in a little rain; an unusually early harvest followed, beginning on September 27 in fine weather.

The *grand cru* wines will keep well. The late-vintage and Sélection des Grains Nobles wines will need considerable time to develop. Hailed as one of the greatest vintages ever.

The lesser wines are delicious now. The great late-harvest and SGN wines 1994 to beyond 2000.

1988★★★ to ★★★★★

The excellent weather throughout the spring and summer raised hopes for a good vintage. However, heavy rains before the harvest disappointed many growers: as much as 50mm (2 inches) fell the weekend before picking.

For some growers, particularly those with well-drained sites, drier weather during the first week of the harvest saved the day. These areas produced some very good wines, including the top Rieslings and Tokay Pinot Gris'. Some excellent late-harvest *Botrytis* styles.

All but the top class late-harvest wines are perfect now. Wines like Schlumberger's Cuvée Anne impressive but very powerful and demanding considerable bottle-age, 1996–2000.

1987★ to ★★★

Following a poor summer, the warm, sunny autumn saved this vintage from disaster.

These are light wines, lacking the structure necessary to age; some of the late-ripening Rieslings will develop complexity, but on the whole this vintage is for early drinking.

All but the grand cru *and special* cuvée *wines should have been consumed by now.*

1986 at best ★★★★

A very good, if slightly uneven vintage. An extremely cold, snowy winter was followed by a more temperate spring, providing excellent conditions for the flowering. Late July saw hail, and bad weather continued until September. Harvesting began late October/early November in misty, sunny, *Botrytis*-inducing weather.

Growers who selected grapes carefully during the harvest produced some excellent wines, particularly the Rieslings which have aged well.

All fully mature. Drink soon.

1985★★★★

A huge crop of good wines. After a cold, wet winter and spring, with a particularly cool spell in April, conditions were fine and dry for the entire summer. The flowering was excellent and picking began in early October, continuing into December for the Sélection des Grains Nobles.

This vintage was very much an all-round success. Some excellent wines were produced, including Gewurztraminers:

good for early drinking. Those suitable for laying down were also of fine quality, including some Rieslings and good late-harvest wines.

Lovely results at each end of the spectrum but only the top SGN and Vendange Tardive wines warrant further bottle-age.

1984★

This was a dull year in Alsace. A mild spring was followed by a cool, wet summer and autumn. A dry October saved the day and the harvest yielded an average crop of wines, thin however, and lacking in fruit. The best were the light Rieslings and Pinot Blancs. Very few late-harvest wines were made.

Drink up.

1983★★★★★

An abundant crop of excellent wines throughout Alsace.

A very warm winter, wet spring and dry summer which lasted into November, enabling growers to pick late into the month.

These were big, rounded, opulent, spicy wines, if occasionally a little overblown. The Gewurztraminer and Tokay are delightful and the top Rieslings worth laying down. 1983 was also an excellent year for the late-harvest wines and Sélection des Grains Nobles.

Lesser wines drink up. The best late-harvest wines are perfection now, yet firm enough for another decade.

1982★★

Apart from a cold spell in January, the weather was fine throughout the year. Picking began on October 7 and yielded one of the largest crops ever: 50% up from the previous year. The results were of low quality. With the exception of some of the better *cuvées*, they were flat, dull wines which tended to lack concentration.

Drink up.

1981★★★★

A good year throughout Alsace. The yields were high and this balanced out stocks after the small 1980 harvest.

High humidity in the earlier part of the vintage gave way to dry, sunny weather during the flowering. This lasted throughout summer until a hot, humid period in early September. The harvest took place in good conditions from late September onwards.

These were, with the exception of some light, inferior Sylvaner, well-balanced, attractive, fruity wines. An excellent late-harvest vintage.

One of the least-known of the really good vintages. Worth looking out for. Undervalued yet at their peak now.

1980★

1980 produced a small quantity of varied though generally low quality wines. Bad weather during the flowering, which reduced the Muscat and Gewurztraminer, was followed by an indifferent summer. Harvest took place during early October in fine weather.

Drink up.

1979★★

After a cool spring, the vines flowered in warm weather. Below average temperatures in July picked up in August and fine weather continued through to the harvest. Grapes were picked from October 30 until late November.

The wines were of good commercial quality but tended to lack acidity; suitable for early drinking.

Drink up.

1978★★

Fruit set was incomplete following a prolonged flowering in a cold June. Consequently the harvest, which took place from late October until mid-November, yielded a small crop. Some quite good wines produced. The Rieslings and Tokays from the top sites had high acidity levels and therefore kept well.

One or two of the late-harvest wines remain and are still beautiful to drink.

1977★

A large vintage; its size was not, however, matched by good quality. Poor weather in spring delayed bud-break, and was followed by an indifferent summer. Picking began late October. At best the wines were steely and austere; the worst were thin and acidic.

Few to be seen. Avoid.

1976★★★★★

After a cold, snowy winter, vines flowered during hot, dry weather in mid-June. The sunny, dry weather continued throughout the summer with the occasional rain shower in July and early October. Harvesting began early in October in good conditions and an average size crop was picked.

Excellent wines with depth and concentration which, after a rather aggressive youth, have matured well. 1976 was also a vintage for the late-harvest wines and Sélection des Grains Nobles, which are still superb.

Minor wines drink up. Most Vendanges Tardives now fully mature though the great SGNs will continue beyond 2000.

1975★★★

After a fine spring the weather was warm and humid for flowering. Conditions were fine throughout the summer and the harvest began in late October.

This was an average sized crop which produced some good wines, particularly the Riesling and Gewurztraminer, though others, especially the Muscats, lacked acidity. The vast majority however, should have been drunk by the end of the 1970s.

Drink up.

1974★

A disappointing year. After a mild, dry winter, bud-break took place in early April but further development was halted by freezing temperatures. The summer was mainly dry and growers forecast an excellent harvest. Hopes were dashed by non-stop drizzle for 30 days. This was the only year when October resulted in no increase in sugar levels. A small crop of poor wines was produced.

Avoid.

1973★★★

After a mild winter, a cool, dry spring with bud-break in late April and a good flowering in mid-June. A splendid summer followed with very little rain from the flowering through to the harvest, which began during the second week of October. Grapes for the late-harvest wines were gathered in by mid-November. The huge size of the crop would now be illegal, but did, nevertheless, produce good Gewurztraminers, attractive Muscats and dry but short Rieslings.

Even the best late-picked wines are passing their peak.

1972

A disappointing year. Bud-break took place in mid-April, after which there was cool weather during May and June and a perfect flowering which began June 20. Hot, dry weather from early July to early August was followed by heavy rain and cold winds causing drought and unusually low temperatures. Maturation was inhibited and the large crop of grapes produced poor, thin, acidic wines.

Avoid.

1971★★★★★

The smallest vintage of the 1970s. Cool, misty weather in June caused *coulure* among some of the Muscats and even the Gewurztraminers but overall the very dry weather, which ran through spring, summer and autumn, produced some excellent late-harvest wines and Sélection des Grains Nobles (the Gewurztraminers were especially good). High temperatures during fermentation necessitated careful control. This was a vintage which rewarded the careful winemakers well.

Most are now past best but fine, rich, late-harvest wines can still be good, though only the finest SGNs will survive longer.

1970★★

After a late bud-break, June was wet and flowering began towards the end of the month, marred slightly by *coulure*. Thereafter the weather was generally fine and picking began in mid-October and finished during the first week of November. A large crop of very ripe, commercial wines that tended to lack the acidity needed for long-ageing.

Few remain. Drink up.

OTHER GOOD/GREAT VINTAGES

1967★★★★, 1964★★★★, 1961★★★★★, 1959★★★★★, 1952★★★★, 1949★★★★, 1947★★★★, 1945★★★★★, 1937★★★★★, 1921★★★★★. Only the rare dessert whites with a high Oechsle reading, well stored, will have survived.

GERMANY

THE WINES OF GERMANY HAVE MANY VIRTUES: they are immediately enjoyable; one does not have to be a great connoisseur to appreciate them; they can be drunk young, fresh and fruity and do not require a big investment and long cellaring; they are light and generally low in alcohol; and even fine wines from the best estates are not expensive – indeed, about the best value in terms of price and intrinsic quality of any of the world's wines.

Yet, apart from cheap, fairly innocuous QbAs – wines of lesser quality to which sugar has been added before fermentation – which sell in large quantities in supermarkets and off licences, the finer wines do not have the following they deserve. There are several reasons: first the labels and names appear, at first sight, to be dauntingly complicated, yet they are logical and more informative than most; second, they are not, apart from the new *Trocken* (dry) wines, food wines, they are best drunk by themselves, not with meals; third, and most worrying, there is understandable confusion: a commercial Niersteiner Domthal sounding much like a Niersteiner Pettenthal of, say, *Auslese* quality from a great estate, inhibits the price that the latter can charge – a short term advantage for the consumer but, long term, not the best inducement for quality wines to be made.

Vintages are important. Indeed, being a relatively northerly European wine region, weather conditions are by no means as reliably satisfactory as more sunny, southerly areas. There is less sunshine, lower natural grape sugars and higher acidity – factors all of which the experienced grower turns to advantage, making wine of delicacy and charm, striving for a perfect balance of fruit and acidity.

The harvest may take place in stages: early picked bunches suitable for chaptalisation, later-picked, riper, bunches for *Spätlese* and *Auslese* qualities, then, if the autumn sunshine persists, with beneficial morning mists, very ripe, sugar-laden grapes affected by *Botrytis* are individually picked to make superlative sweet *Beerenauslesen* and intensely concentrated *Trockenbeerenauslesen* (TBAs). Hopefully, in most vintages light, agreeable wines will be made for drinking soon after bottling, usually the spring after the harvest.

The vintage notes that follow are more concerned with the higher grades of wine; the better the vintage, the finer the wines and the longer they will keep. It is a mistake to think that all German wines should be drunk young. The top quality wines, *Auslese* and above, actually need and improve with bottle-age. Many '71s are just approaching their peak; some of the great '37s are still miraculously lovely.

1991 ★★ to ★★★★

After the unprecedented successes of the previous three vintages it would be easy to dismiss 1991 as a failure. This is not so, though the results are highly variable, depending on the district and the times of picking. In any case, after so much quality wine, a large harvest of QbAs should prove very useful commercially.

In the Saar and Ruwer, the severe frost of April 20/21 halved the crop. Perversely, this increased the concentration of the remaining grapes and enabled them to survive the summer drought that affected most other regions, inhibiting ripening. There was also frost as late as early June, but flowering, though delayed, was generally successful. The weather remained hot and dry until mid-September, those vineyards on water retentive soils, such as the eastern parts of the Rheingau, survived better than those on light sandy soils, as in the Rheinpfalz. Hail in August decimated some areas of the Rheinhessen.

Because of the weather conditions, picking time was critical. The rain was too late, and optimum harvesting conditions only lasted for one week. Those who picked before October 27 and after November 4 missed out. Nevertheless in certain districts *Botrytis* was taken advantage of, and some growers in the middle Mosel managed to make wine at every quality rung up to *Trockenbeerenauslese*. An *Eiswein* from the Ruländer grape was, for the first time, made at Castell in Franconia on December 13.

Inexpensive QbA wines, drink now (all brands of Liebfraumilch can be drunk as soon as they appear on supermarket shelves or merchants' lists). Even the Kabinett *and* Spätlese *quality wines can be drunk within the next year or so. The rarer* Auslesen *will have the acidity to develop over, say, 3 to 5 years and the even rarer, and expensive,* Beerenauslesen *and TBAs from 1996 to either side of the turn of the century.*

1990★★★★

An excellent vintage; never before has Germany had three consecutive years of top quality wines, although everywhere quantities were down on 1989.

Leaf development was very early but stopped for two weeks during a very cold April. May was mainly warm and dry, accompanied by occasional hailstorms and showers. And the very cold, sometimes freezing nights extended blossoming over almost four weeks, particularly in the south. The result was incomplete fertilisation or 'blossom-drop' and irregular development of the small berries.

Berries remained small throughout the hot, dry summer, and the heavy rain in late August, followed by storms in many areas, resulted in rot which reduced the crop size.

Picking was very advanced for the early varieties, many of which made wines in the *Prädikat* range. Everywhere this was described as an 'ideal' autumn. Contrary to expectation, acidity was higher than in the '89s and many growers felt that this would be the firmer, better, more consistent vintage of the trio.

A classic Riesling vintage: some estates reported harvesting only *Spätlese* and *Auslese*-quality Riesling with excellent acidity, and in the Rheingau the wines promise to store well. Growers from Baden were optimistic for excellent red wines. The only disappointments were in the Saar and Ruwer where the grapes were less ripe and *Botrytis* did not develop well, consequently few late-harvest dessert wines were made.

Minor wines drinking now, those of Spätlese *and* Auslese *quality from now to well into the 20th century.*

1989★★★★★

A huge vintage of excellent wines, twinned with 1988: the latter being firm, and the '89s having grace and charm. An average of 50% of the crop was declared as *Prädikat* wine, and this increased to as much as 66% in the Rheingau.

Near perfect weather prevailed throughout the year. A mild winter and warm spring prompted an early bud-break, followed by flowering in ideal conditions.

The summer was warm and dry, only interrupted by occasional thunder and hailstorms, the effects of which were severe but very localised. Meanwhile, the grapes ripened well and picking began early at the beginning of September.

Most growers selected carefully, and so avoided the usual disappointments associated with overproduction. The Rheingau enjoyed the best vintage there since 1971: the grapes had benefited from elevated *Botrytis* levels and made highly concentrated wines. A classic Riesling vintage.

All can be drunk now but the better quality Prädikat *wines will improve in bottle until the end of the century.*

1988★★★★

Excellent summer weather prompted hopes that this would be a classic year for German wines. However, unfortunate pre-harvest rain, fog and, in the Saar and Ruwer, hail, dampened expectations, but did not prevent this from being a good vintage.

In the Middle Mosel the weather remained fine throughout the harvest and some classic *Auslese* wines were made, especially in the region between Erden and Bernkastel. Many of these will last well.

Frosts during the harvest in the Nahe on November 7 enabled growers to make superb *Eiswein*.

Rheinhessen and the Rheinpfalz produced some good wines, the top *Prädikats* being real classics. Perhaps the weakest wines came from the Rheingau, but even here many still reached *Kabinett* standard.

QbA and Kabinett *wines need drinking but* Auslesen, *though delicious now, will keep well, say to 1998.*

1987

A severe winter, during which temperatures sank to −15°C (5°F) causing some damage to the vines. April was warm but temperatures fell again during May and June and heavy rain caused rot in some areas. Considerable pessimism resulted from this – one renowned Mosel grower declared that he would not be bottling his '87s at all.

Warm, dry weather from mid-September until the harvest alleviated much anxiety. The Rieslings were harvested from October 28, although many growers held off for as long as possible so that picking continued until the end of November.

The crop was quite large, but of this only 15% was *Qualitätswein mit Prädikat* (high quality wine), the majority being only QbA.

Drink up.

1986★ to ★★★

Problems caused by difficult harvest conditions made this a vintage of mixed quality. An exceptionally severe winter, during which temperatures fell as low as −20°C (−4°F) was followed by a mild spring, then warm weather during May and June. Flowering was early, starting mid-June.

The hot summer gave way to a poor September but this did not dispel optimism among growers for a good harvest.

However, violent storms in late October stripped vines and made harvesting difficult.

Those sites which had escaped the storms produced some excellent, top-quality wines. The best were the *Auslesen*, *Beerenauslesen* and the *Trockenbeerenauslesen* produced in the Rheinpfalz. Elsewhere the wines were of average quality.

Drink up all but the top quality wines, the sweetest capable of lasting a further 10 years or more.

1985★★★

Severe frosts and hail during the winter considerably pruned the eventual size of the crop, but as is often the case, the quality was generally high.

In the Mosel flowering took place in late June and poor weather continued until September. An Indian summer saved the day, providing good conditions for late ripening, and the harvest began on November 17. The better sites here made some excellent, well-structured, acidic wines which will last well.

After a poor start to the year the Rheingau enjoyed more even weather conditions than the Mosel; the summer was hot and dry and picking began November 4. The dry weather reduced the size of the crop and winemakers produced some excellent wines. At worst, sometimes dull, short, lacking.

Most are delicious to drink now and really should be consumed. Only the very best worth hanging on to.

1984

A cool spring delayed flowering until mid-July. Vine growth was on average three weeks behind normal, and problems were exacerbated by poor weather throughout the summer. The harvest started in late October for the lesser grape varieties and mid-November for the Riesling. The grapes were unripe and the wines were excessively acidic.

If you still have some, drink up, otherwise avoid.

1983★★★

The year got off to a bad start with a cool, wet spring which caused flooding along the Rhine and Mosel. Fortunately, the vines were not damaged and fine, warm weather in June hastened growth. Flowering took place at the end of the month.

The excessively wet spring was counterbalanced by one of the hottest, driest summers on record. The early-harvest grapes were picked in September. A period of rain followed by sun then swelled and ripened the Rieslings and picking for these began later in October. Virtually no *Edelfäule*.

The wines of 1983 combine quality with quantity. Over 40% of the huge crop was of *Prädikat* standard. The best since 1976. Those from Saar and Ruwer and the Nahe fared best.

Take advantage of a very attractive vintage, an all round success: delicious wines, the top grades will keep.

1982★

A huge vintage – the biggest ever recorded in Germany – producing 165 million cases. The quality, however, did not match the quantity.

Fine, warm weather during spring encouraged an early

flowering during the first week of June. The gloriously hot summer prompted much optimism among growers, but hopes were dispelled by wet weather in early October which diluted the grapes and caused rot.

About 22% of the wines were of *Prädikat* quality, the top sites producing some very good results, the best coming from the steep, well-drained sites of the Mosel where the Riesling grape (which resists rot well) thrives.

Drink up.

1981★★

A warm spring prompted early growth. Unfortunately, progress was checked by severe April frosts which damaged the newly grown shoots – most seriously in the Rheingau and the Saar and Ruwer areas.

May and June were warm and wet, and flowering began fairly early (June 8) but was interrupted by rain causing damage in all areas, particularly in the Rheingau.

The remaining crop ripened well in good weather during the last part of the summer, only to encounter the hazards of rains during late September/early October. The Rieslings were picked from October 12 and growers who held out longer and harvested later were rewarded by drier weather occuring towards the end of the month.

This was a small crop of mixed quality wines. The best were the fresh, racy *Kabinette* and *Spätlesen* from the Mosel.

There is life-supporting acidity and tart acidity. The '81s have a lot of both. The better Kabinett *and* Spätlese *quality wines can still be attractive. But drink up.*

1980

A disastrous year for German wines. A cold wet winter, cool spring, lovely warm weather through May to early June, then wet weather and the latest flowering in memory, finishing at the end of July. The vines also suffered severe *coulure*. Poor weather throughout the summer prevented the grapes from ripening and picking was delayed until early November. This, though, enabled winemakers to produce a reasonable amount of *Prädikat* wine (30% of output in all) but overall, this was a thin, hard vintage.

Few remain. Avoid or drink up.

1979★★★

Light, easy, enjoyable wines. Severe January frosts, following a hard winter, caused widespread damage to the dormant vines. The full effects were seen only in May, especially in the Mosel-Saar-Ruwer and parts of the Rheinhessen. The Rieslings, however, did not suffer greatly and the Mosel produced some good wines.

A largely forgotten vintage, many very attractive wines were made which, thanks to good acidity levels, are still delicious for drinking.

1978★★

Bad weather during the spring, a late flowering and wet summer weather finally gave way to a fine, dry, sunny September which pruned the crop, especially in the Mosel. Harvest was late.

Pleasant enough wines but lacking in length.

Drink up.

1977★

A mediocre, rather uninteresting year. The vines started well but flowering was hampered by a cold April and May. The summer was changeable but generally inclement until a delightful October. Conditions were ideal for the development of *Edelfäule* (noble rot) amongst the Rieslings, and a small quantity of *Eiswein* was made. Some passable wines from the southerly Rheinpfalz, but all past their best.

Avoid, or drink up.

1976★★★★

A gloriously ripe vintage. In northern Europe exceptional heat throughout the summer produced delightful wines. Blossoming and growth was extremely early – by as much as three weeks along the banks of the Rhine and Mosel. Late August rain swelled the grapes; September to mid-October was warm and then damper conditions encouraged the spread of noble rot among the late-ripening grapes.

1976 produced a fairly small crop of fruity, well-balanced wines. The best year since 1971, perhaps less ripe than the '71s and less fat than the '64s and the '59s, but very appealing. Many *Auslesen*, *Beeren-* and *Trockenbeerenauslesen*, all lovely, the best with time in hand, some, though, lack acidity.

Drink now. Most are fully mature and will not benefit from further bottle-age.

1975★★★★

Except for a cold April, the weather was warm, flowering speedy and successful, and summer was hot, culminating in a scorching August. Early September was wet but autumn sun ripened the grapes for the harvest beginning on October 17.

An undervalued year, the trade being more interested in the '76s as soon as they came onto the market. The '75s, being firmer and more acidic, have, however, eventually overtaken the '76s. A vintage also notable for increasingly widespread use of new grape varieties and unusual crossings. Those of *Auslese* quality still lovely.

Upstaged at every turn by the '76s, yet more than holding their own. Even after this time the best are still delicious and, if you can find them, go for a song.

1974

A dreary, wet vintage. Heavy rains during harvest time washed out the crop.

Few seen. Avoid.

1973★★

The largest crop on record. A late spring was followed by an unusually hot summer, some September rain and then more sun until November. The wines were of variable quality, ranging from some very pleasant examples which, however, lacked acidity and extract (perhaps due to overproduction), to uninteresting. A vintage for quick drinking.

Should have been drunk in the mid- to late 1970s. Too late now except for a few perfect Eisweins.

1972★

An unexciting year that nevertheless produced useful commercial wine which restocked the trade cellars depleted after the sales of the outstanding '71s.

Few if any remain. Avoid.

1971★★★★★

A magnificent, classic year of great abundance. So great that traders bemoaned the lack of commercial wines in their cellars.

The vines flowered early and well, then a wonderfully sunny summer lasted right through to the autumn. The resulting grapes were small, ripe, well-nourished and immensely healthy. Best of all were the grapes from the Mosel which had absorbed the moisture from the early-morning autumn mists.

They were soft, delicious wines with a perfect balance of ripe sweetness and fruit acidity. They had none of the flaccid quality of the '64s or the almost overwhelming richness of the '59s, but were closer in weight and charm to the '53s and '49s.

Spätlese *and below are showing signs of fatigue so drink up. But* Auslesen *and the great dessert wines are not only delicious now but will continue to evolve.*

1970★★

A mediocre year. The vines blossomed late and a dry summer followed. Those who picked late were able to make high-quality wines; some picking continued right through to December and even January, enabling *Eiswein* to be made. Some good wines but they were overshadowed by the '71s. Of little interest now.

Just a few quality wines holding on, but, on balance, drink up.

1969 at best ★★★

After a satisfactory summer which prompted optimism among winemakers, a dry September failed to swell the berries, then a dense fog prevented the sun from penetrating the grapes. Those who had to pick early suffered, especially in the Palatinate and the Rheinhessen, but in the Rheingau and the Mosel the Rieslings benefited from some late autumn sun. The best were good, firm wines, especially in the Mosel. Forgotten once the '71s arrived. Some still worth seeking out.

Some excellent hochfeine Auslesen *from the Mosel, otherwise drink up.*

1968

An abundant quantity of poor-quality wines. The odd surprise.
None remain, thank goodness.

1967★ to ★★★★★

After a mild winter the spring suffered a combination of sun, rain, terrible cold, wind and thunderstorms. Summer was better but disastrous harvest rain washed out some districts. Those who delayed picking were able to enjoy some late Autumn sun and made excellent *Trockenbeerenauslesen*.

The results ranged from a few poor, thin wines to some excellent dessert wines. The top estates are still worth looking out for: excellent and underrated.

Happily all the lesser wines will have been consumed by now but the TBAs are still magisterial, Wagnerian.

1966★★★

Good, stylish wines. Few dessert wines were made owing to cold wet weather in early November which delayed late harvesting and limited further ripening. However, a few *Eiswein*s were made with some success.

Overall, pale, firm, steely wines with sustaining acidity, but lacking ripeness.

Over the top now. Drink up.

1965

With the odd exception, an unusually bad year due to uneven weather conditions.

Happily none to be found now.

1964★★★★

The best vintage of the 1960s, much welcomed and very popular, coming after four rather uninteresting years.

Fine, dry weather continued right through the spring and summer pushing the growth of the vines ahead of normal. The lack of rain coupled with an increase in production in some areas caused some concern among growers. Ultimately, an enormous crop was harvested and picking continued through to the end of November.

The finest and longest-lasting wines were those from the northerly, steep, slate slopes of the Mosel-Saar-Ruwer where the acidity counterbalanced the unusually high sweetness of the grapes. Overall, these were soft, ripe wines. The best vintage between 1959 and 1971.

All but the very best wines from the Mosel-Saar-Ruwer tiring now. The latter, from top estates, can still be lovely.

1963★ to ★★★

Very cold weather continued throughout the winter and spring months, giving way to delightful conditions in July. The next three months were wet, followed by an Indian summer at the end of October.

Overall, there were roughly equal quantities of below- and above-average wines, which, considering the weather conditions, was a success. The Mosel did not fare well.

Minor wines long since past best. The better quality wines drying out.

1962★★

A year which included a long cold spell and a long period of drought. However, those who delayed harvesting were rewarded by a change in the weather. Picking continued into December

and much *Eiswein* was made. These were the best '62s. The rest being pleasant but very light.
All but the Eiswein *long since faded.*

1961★ to ★★

A moderate vintage.

Following a good spring, but a poor summer, September saved the day with record temperatures and uninterrupted sunshine. A small crop of very uneven quality wines was produced, and which achieved, but perhaps did not merit, very high prices. No great sweet wines.
Few remain. Drink up.

1960★

A large crop of raw, unripe, too-soft wines. The best came from the Palatinate.
Few if any remain; not worth seeking.

1959★★★★★

An outstanding vintage. Rarely has such a prolific crop produced such consistently high quality wines.

An exceptionally fine summer: hot, dry weather right through to October. The vines were extremely healthy and, with only a few exceptions, the grapes were gathered in successfully. Anxiety was caused by the almost unprecedented heat at vintage time, the unusually high sugar content and low acidity of the grapes, though only the less-skilled winemakers encountered problems as a result of this.

Overall, these were excellent, full-bodied, naturally sweet, ripe wines which developed slowly. A record number of *Beeren-* and *Trockenbeerenauslen* were made in the Mosel-Saar-Ruwer districts.
As in Burgundy, the last of the heavy-weight vintages. Many great wines from Auslese *to TBA are still superb to drink. The latter will keep.*

1958★★

A huge crop – the biggest for 20 years – of moderate quality wines. Few were imported and few tasted. Rather dull, and over-acid in style.
All consumed.

1957★★

Early growth was badly damaged by heavy May frosts. A good summer was followed by rain throughout September, inflicting rot in some areas. Some good *Kabinett* wines were produced in the Mosel where the late-ripening Rieslings benefited from good weather in October.

Wines which were mostly consumed by the early 1960s.
Few remain. Avoid.

1956

A disastrous, cold, wet year. Small quantity, very low quality.
None tasted.

1955★★

A moderate, rather uninteresting vintage. Apart from eight weeks of fine weather from mid-July, bad conditions prevailed throughout the year with frosts in mid-October, a week before the harvest began. With few exceptions, a small crop of uneven, commercial wines.
Drink up.

1954

Very poor quality wines due to appalling weather conditions.

1953★★★★★

An outstanding vintage – the result of good weather throughout the year except for some severe frosts in May which damaged the vines in the lower grade areas. Healthy grapes were harvested in excellent, sunny conditions.

Wines from the Rheingau reached perfection; they were elegant, firm and supple. Many which were soft and pleasant, not meant to last, were produced in the Mosel; the best coming from the Saar and Ruwer. Open-knit, easy wines were made in the Rheinhessen, the Silvaner grape producing the best. Overall, a ripe and fruity vintage which varied in character from district to district.

NB The quality of corks used in the mid-1950s was poor, some failing to withstand the test of time.

Only the feinste Auslese *to TBA have survived, the lesser wines well past best. The solitary survivors can, however, be glorious.*

1952★★★

Fine weather prevailed throughout the summer, including scorching sun in July/August. This would have been an outstanding vintage had it not been for two months of rain in September/October.

Well-constituted wines were made in what turned out to be an underrated vintage; most of them were consumed in the mid- to late 1950s.

Firm wines with good acidity, some of which still retain a certain freshness as well as honeyed bottle-age.

1951

A poor, thin year.

1950★★

A pleasant year of commercial quality. Inevitably it stood in the shadow of 1949.

Very rarely seen and not worth seeking out.

1949★★★★★

A great classic year – the best Mosel since 1921 – which happily coincided with renewed post-war market demand. Apart from early spring frosts, which pruned the crop size, the weather conditions were excellent. These were firm, well-balanced,

refined wines which lasted well.
The top quality wines still delicious.

1948★★

Sandwiched between two superior years, this average vintage did not attract much interest. Few shipped. None seen.

1947★★★★

Severe winter frosts hardened the soil, preventing moisture from penetrating. A warm, dry summer followed, producing an average sized crop. These conditions produced grapes which lacked the moisture necessary for full ripening. The wines were low in acidity and short-lived. They were nevertheless soft, rich and of high quality.
TBAs from the great Rheingau estates are still magnificent.

1946★★

Ignored by the trade who unfairly categorised this an 'off' vintage.

1945★★★★★

Coming at the end of the war, the vines suffered from disease and a lack of labour to combat it. There was also much looting by released Polish and Russian prisoners. Consequently, despite the fine summer, a tiny crop was harvested. However, those that were made were excellent.
Now drying out and tired.

1943★★

The best of the wartime vintages.
Beerenauslesen *still remarkably good.*

1930s

The 1930s produced some interesting vintages, although after 1937 German wines were rarely seen abroad.
1937★★★★ was magnificent: an early flowering, a hot, dry summer and September rain, which swelled the grapes, made this the best year since 1921. My favourite German vintage. The best can still be fabulously good.
The second-best year of the 1930s was **1934★★★★** some wines even merited five stars. Few to be found now and likely to be over the top.
1933★★★ produced an abundant crop of soft wines; some Rheingaus were still holding well in 1978, demonstrating how natural, unsugared, well-cellared wine can still be delightful at 45 years of age.
The first three years of the decade were, sadly, of poor quality.

1920s

With the exception of a few good years, the decade was not overall as satisfactory as in the main French districts.
1929★★★★ was the first really good vintage since 1921.

Spring frosts were followed by a hot, dry summer which lasted well into September, a small crop of healthy, ripe grapes was harvested. If cellared carefully, these wines lasted well, but now are very rare.

1925★★★ was a good, though rarely seen vintage, but the best vintage of the decade was undoubtedly **1921**★★★★★ arguably the greatest vintage of the century. Spring frosts and a summer drought reduced the size of the crop and disease-free grapes were picked in good conditions. Those from the Mosel and the Rhine were the best and even some of the minor wines can still be interesting to drink.

1920★★★ produced variable but mainly good wines. Some late-vintage wines were outstanding.

1910s

1915★★★ produced a good, abundant vintage, as in Burgundy and Champagne. **1911**★★★★★ was an excellent year, particularly for the wines from the Rheingau: the end of an era.

1900s

1906★ was a modest vintage. The next best year prior to 1911 was **1900**★★★★ an excellent vintage, considered by some even better than 1893.

1890s

A decade which included a moderately good vintage in **1895**★★ and an excellent vintage in **1893**★★★★★ – probably the best of the century. A small quantity of very rich wines was made following an exceptionally hot summer.

AUSTRIA

MOZART, STRAUSS, VIENNA, AND THE DANUBE; mountains for skiing and The Sound of Music. All most evocative. And wines to match, though surprisingly little known outside Austria despite their easy-to-drink charm and reasonable prices. Apart from the over-publicised and unfortunate so-called 'anti-freeze' scandal in the early 1980s, excellent wines have been made here, traditionally in the Wachau, Burgenland on the Hungarian border, Styria in the south, and around Vienna – the only major European capital city to have such a wealth of vines on its doorstep.

Although red wines are produced it is the light, dry to medium-dry white wines of Germanic style that are the best known: Riesling, Müller-Thurgau, the highly scented Muskat Ottonel, Traminer, Ruländer, Weissburgunder (Pinot Blanc) and the popular, soft and fruity Grüner Veltliner, best drunk young. Excellent late-harvest wines are made, rich *Auslesen* and outstanding '*Ausbruch*', the latter a cross between a five or six *putt* Tokay and *Beerenauslese* from the Palatinate.

As with most other white wines, the lighter, drier styles should be drunk within a year or so of the vintage (though the Viennese flock out to the suburbs to drink the new wine shortly after it has finished fermenting), only the finer late-harvest *Auslese* to *Trockenbeerenauslese*-type wines having a good cellar life.

1991★

Bitterly cold winter and late spring. The flowering was also delayed by cool weather and a poor June. July was warm and sunny but August was heralded by torrential rain causing flooding of cellars and low lying vineyards. The latter half of August was fine but the vines were too far retarded, the harvest being delayed and hampered by wet weather and rot. Nevertheless in Burgenland, growers who waited took advantage of a late Indian summer, and, around Rust, made some exceptional *Botrytis*-affected sweet wines.

Best to avoid, or drink soon, the very acidic minor wines. Look out for the richer dessert wines which will be good for drinking 1994–98.

1990★★★★★

After a normal spring, summer brought the same drought which affected large tracts of Europe. Areas of light and sandy soil suffered the most, especially the younger vines where the rootstock was unable to find sufficient water, but irrigated estates (in the Wachau for example) fared well. In general, good winemakers made superlative wines but overall quality can be patchy. Quantities were good.

In the individual regions there were some excellent wines in the Wachau and Kamptal-Donauland, with some good dry *Spätlesen* from most properties. A long autumn allowed good quality Gumpoldskirchners to be produced from the traditional Spätrot-Rotgipfler, including a good many high *Prädikat* wines. The long growing season also came as a god-send to the Styrian growers, for whom cool conditions sometimes prevent the grapes from ripening fully; Sauvignon Blancs and Morillons (Chardonnays) were particularly fine. In the Burgenland there were many top *Prädikat* wines made, including some *Ausbruch*. In the Weinviertel one grower even picked an *Eiswein* on the first day of the Gulf War.

Minor whites, Grüner Veltliner, drink now. Late-picked quality whites benefiting from a little bottle-age, drinking now to 1996; the dessert wines will keep longer.

1989★★

A mild winter was succeeded by a cold, damp spring. The summer was variable with frequent rain. Finally, in mid-October, a period of good sunny weather set in and lasted until the first days of November. The variable quality of the vintage put paid to hopes of another superlative 'niner' (an old peasant tradition in Austria holds that the best years for wine are those ending in nine), but growers who picked late made very good wines, particularly in Burgenland and Styria. In the Thermenregion* many of the wines have a musty character, evidence that not all of the grapes used were sound.

Drink up all but the best late-picked wines.

1988★★

1988 was the first year in five not to be affected by severe frosts. The result was a potentially bumper crop. A good spring was followed by a hot summer, but the rain came in September. Those who picked early may have made wines on the dilute side, others were rewarded by an Indian summer. Quality is therefore variable.

The vintage seems to have been best in Lower Austria, where the rare Roter Veltliner grape did exceptionally well. One grower in Langenlois harvested an *Eiswein* as early as November 5. Many Styrian wines betray a taste of rot.

Drink now.

1987★

After a generally abominable year in the vineyards a good autumn came to the rescue and in general the '87s are good if occasionally on the sharp side. One or two excellent red wines were made in Burgenland.

Drink up.

1986★★★★★

Before 1990, 1986 was considered the best vintage in Austria since 1979. One or two Austrian wine-writers even came out with that dangerous phrase 'the vintage of the century'.

Frost damage reduced the size of the crop to below average, but otherwise growing conditions were near perfect. The wines to look out for are the reds from Burgenland, Styrian wines, and Wachau Rhine Rieslings. High *Spätlesen* were harvested in the Weinviertel and one or two *Auslesen* in Vienna. One grower in Langenlois even picked a Grüner Veltliner on October 5 and fermented it in new oak! The wines are high in extract and have good acidity.

The best dry whites, from low-yielding vineyards, firm and acidic and at their peak now.

---

* South of Vienna, encompassing Baden and Gumpoldskirchen.

1985★★★★

Spring frosts killed off up to 95% of vines in parts of the Weinviertel, and elsewhere in Austria the damage ensured that the harvest was not even half the average. The flowering also took place under exceedingly difficult conditions but the rest of the year was good, if not excellent: 'a great year' as one Langenlois uttered perversely.

There were some very good reds from the Burgenland, impressive, long-living Sauvignon Blancs from Styria; and a small amount of botrytised wine was produced in the Thermenregion.

An attractive vintage, but most at peak if not tiring. The reds are worth seeking out.

1984★★★

Originally thought of as the post-war *annus mirabilis*, but later denigrated for a lack of acidity in the wines. Near perfect weather in summer and autumn led to a large crop. Growers who ensured that their wines had sufficient acidic backbone produced wines with the best vintage potential.

In the Burgenland, 1984 produced the best quality reds to emerge before the 1990 vintage. Elsewhere areas not normally noted for *Prädikat* wines yielded musts high in residual sugar; there were *Auslesen* in Styria and the Weinviertel, and high *Spätlesen* in the Wachau. Naturally, most of these were vinified as dry wines.

Drink up.

1983★★★★★

A great vintage. Outstandingly ripe wines, notably excellent *Trockenbeerenauslesen*.

All the soft, dry whites should have been drunk by now but the exceedingly sweet and concentrated TBAs are still superb and will keep.

1982★ to ★★★

The biggest crop on record. An excellent summer and early autumn was rounded off with a miserable, wet October. Those who picked before (or after) the rain, produced wines of quality.

Good levels of *Botrytis cinerea* in the Thermenregion. Some luscious *Prädikat* wines from Rust.

The top class sweet whites at peak.

1981★★★

Notable only for late-picked sweet wines. These were quite widespread, with wines of *Trockenbeerenauslese* levels in Rust and the Seewinkel; high *Prädikats* in the Thermenregion; one or two rare *Ausbruch* wines from Vienna; and the rarest of all: *Beerenauslese*, from Styria.

Ausbrüche *and TBAs still excellent and will keep.*

1980

A bad year pretty well everywhere.

Avoid.

1979★★★★★

An excellent year which began with a perfect flowering and continued through a hot summer and a sunny autumn. The last of the great 'niners'. Most of the '79s have now been consumed. The long autumn produced *Auslese* levels in the Wachau and Krems, *Beerenauslese* in Styria, *Ausbruch* in Vienna and Klosterneuberg, and *Trockenbeerenauslese* in Rust and the Seewinkel.

Drink up all but the top dessert wines, which have excellent acidity and long life.

1978★

A cold, dry vintage; generally mediocre.
Drink up.

1977★★★★

Excellent year with splendid weather extending throughout the growing season: particularly good Rieslings and Grüner Veltliners from Lower Austria.

Few, if any, remain. Drink up.

1976★ to ★★★

Variable weather which improved only in late autumn. Those who picked early made thin, dull wines. Some good *Trockenbeerenauslese* and *Ausbruch* from the Burgenland, a Weisser Burgunder *Beerenauslese* unready at five years of age. This class of wine needs bottle-age.

Drink only the Ausbruch *and TBA which are holding well and can be superb.*

1975★★

Generally average quality only. One or two surprises such as a magnificently racy Pinot Noir from Langenlois.
Drink up.

1974

Generally very poor.
Avoid.

1973★★★★

Very good year, especially for Riesling and Grüner Veltliner grapes in Lower Austria. A long autumn allowed for some *Spätlese* and *Auslese* wines to be made in the Wachau. The Thermenregion made high *Prädikat* wines and good *Trockenbeerenauslese* and *Ausbruch* are occasionally still encountered from the Burgenland. One of the great *Ausbruch* years.

Few remain but the best Auslesen, Ausbrüche *and TBAs worth looking out for.*

1972

A very poor year. Now largely forgotten.
Forget it.

1971★★★★★

Long-lasting wines from an excellent year.
Some top Rieslings from Vienna and even one or two Grüner Veltliners from the Wachau still on top form; also scented, honeyed Beerenauslesen *from Rust.*

1970★★

Not generally a good year. One or two stylish Rieslings from the steeper slopes of Vienna.
Drink up.

MORE REMOTE VINTAGES

1969★★★★★ was one of the great 'niners'; some top *Trockenbeerenauslesen* from Rust can still be found and are superb. 1967★★★ produced good *Prädikats* from the Burgenland: look out for *Ausbrüche* and TBAs; 1966★★★ saw fine Rieslings from lower Austria, some surprisingly good wines from Styria, and rich, fat, powerful TBAs from Langenlois. 1963★★★★ some very attractive *Prädikat* wine from the Burgenland.

Look out for the 1961★★★★★ *raresimme Trockenbeerenauslese* or *Auslese* from the Burgenland; excellent wines were also produced in 1959★★★★★ though all but the richest and best are drying out.

1955~ was chiefly memorable only for the departure of the Allied armies, notably the Russians. 1949★★★★★ was a great year. And 1945★★★★ the year when all the old stocks of Austrian wine disappeared down the throats of the invading Soviet troops.

Older vintages are so rare that one might as well say that they do not exist.

HUNGARY
(TOKAY)

HUNGARY IS A SURPRISINGLY BIG AND SUCCESSFUL wine producing country. Its best known regions, growing red and white table wines, are around Eger and on the slopes bounding Lake Balaton. Until the final disintegration of the Iron Curtain, basically only two qualities were produced, everyday inexpensive quick-consumption wines, and wines of slightly superior quality for the many excellent restaurants and for export. To produce higher quality wines was contrary to Communist Party thinking, for it introduced an exalted price factor linked with privilege. Wines such as Badacsony Riesling and Egri Bikaver (Bull's Blood) in good years are sound and attractive but are essentially for early consumption. Several other local grape varieties are used, making passably appealing wines for a mainly local market.

The odd man out is Tokay. Indeed Tokay is *the* odd man out amongst the great classic wines of Europe. Happily, the quality, though not up to Hapsburg Empire standards, has always been satisfactory (when I visited the region in 1971, however, one could see that the higher, better vineyard slopes had been abandoned and vines were being grown under irrigation on the highly cultivated lower slopes, a situation not conducive to production of the finest wines). Better news for Hungary is that there is a renewed interest in the wines of this region, and outside capital and know-how is moving in.

Tokay makes not only an unusual style of wine, it has quite remarkable ageing potential. Indeed, in common with Madeira, the finest and the richest Tokays have an almost limitless cellar life. For this reason this section of the pocketbook is devoted solely to Tokay vintages.

However, Tokay appears in various guises. Szamorodni or natural table wines can be dry or sweet in style; both, in good vintages, will keep though the dry is something of an acquired taste – as are Portuguese mature white wine and Château-Chalon. The Aszú wines, to which measures of a concentrate made from overripe grapes are added, range from medium-sweet 3 puttonyos to a very sweet, Sauternes-like, 5 puttonyos. Following exceptional years intensely sweet and long-lasting Aszú-Eszencia will be produced (the pure Eszencia or Essence – various spellings – is rare and very expensive but it has an almost limitless life span).

1990s

1991★★ average wines. 1990★★★★ a good all round vintage.

1980s

1989★★★★ very good. 1988★★★★★ one of the two best vintages of the decade. 1987★★ moderate. 1986★★ average. 1985★★ average. 1984★★ average. 1983★★★★★ excellent. 1982★★★★ 1981★★★ and 1980~ a wretched vintage.

1970s

1979★★★★ 1978★ disappointing. 1977~ poor. 1976★★★ 1975★★★★ 1974~ poor. 1973★★★ good Aszú crop. 1972★★★★★ wonderful Aszús: excellent, will keep. 1971★★★★ 1970~

1960s

1969★★★ 1968★★★★★ Aszú-Eszencia lovely, but will develop further. 1967★★ 1966★★★ 1965~ 1964★★★★ the first post-war vintage of Aszú-Eszencia imported and marketed in the UK. 1963★★★★★ the best dry and all the sweet wines drinking well. 1962★★★★ 1961★★★★ 1960~

1950s

1959★★★★★ dry Szamorodni tired but all the sweet wines perfect now. 1958★★★ 1957★★★★★ 1956★★★★ 1955★★★ 1954~ 1953★★★★ 1952★★★★★ 1951~ 1950★★★★

1940s

1949★★★★★ 1948★★★ 1947★★★★★ a perfect Aszú crop; magnificent concentrated Eszencia. 1946★★★ good. 1945★★★ Eszencia. 1944~ 1943★★★ 1942★★★★ 1941~ 1940~

THE BEST PRE-1940 VINTAGES

1937★★★★★ 1936★★★★★ 1935★★★ 1934★★★★★ 1932★★★★★ 1931★★★★★ 1930★★★ 1927★★★★★ 1924★★★★★ 1923★★★★★ 1922★★★ 1921★★★★ 1920★★★★ 1919★★★★★ 1916★★★★★ 1915★★★★★ 1914★★★ 1912★★★★★ 1910★★★ 1907★★★ 1906★★★★★ the last great vintage of the Austro-Hungarian Empire. 1905★★★ 1904★★★★ 1901★★★

Great Tokay Vintages (only the Ausbrüche and Eszencias will have survived): **1889, 1865, 1834, 1811** – the most renowned vintage of all time.

ITALY

FOR SHEER VOLUME OF WINE PRODUCED, AND FOR variations of style and quality, Italy is unmatched. It is also an impossible country to deal with in a general way as climatic conditions vary widely: from Sicily, with its North African influence, to the foothills of the Alps. Classic French grape varieties are starting to intrude, changing the nature of some wines though winemaking methods alternate between primitive and highly sophisticated.

Undependable, less so; unpredictable, perhaps. But there have been enormous strides made in the 1980s. A combination of new attitudes, much improved winemaking and amenable weather conditions have enhanced the quality of Italian wine out of all recognition.

Two major districts have long been, and still are, regarded as the homes of the great Italian classics: Tuscany, with its famous Chianti region, between Florence and Siena, and to the north, Piedmont, producing sturdy long-living Barolo and stylish Barbaresco in the hills around Alba and Asti.

These two districts not only set the standards but, amongst Italian wines exported, are the best known in the quality field, which is why they are featured principally in the vintage notes that follow.

1991★

Piedmont Cold spring, late and irregular flowering, a long hot and very dry summer followed by heavy rain at vintage time. An average crop, variable in quality, mainly light wines.

Tuscany Poor spring, cold and wet with damaging frosts; dismal May to mid-June alternating rain and too little sun. The summer was hearteningly hot and dry but the rains returned for the late harvest. Variable quality, lower than average production.

The light dry whites, particularly the slightly sparkling Moscato d'Asti, can be drunk now. Chianti Classico and Chianti Rufino more quickly developing than the previous three vintages. Barolo, say 1994–98.

1990★★★★★

The hot, dry summer produced grapes of exceptional quality. Yields were very low everywhere and the small bunches of concentrated fruit encouraged growers to predict a top class vintage, ranking beside those of the best in the postwar era.

Piedmont The third year of almost perfect weather conditions in Barolo and Barbaresco. Rainfall was better distributed than in 1988 and beautifully healthy grapes were picked two weeks ahead of normal. The quantity, however, was around 10% down. Promising well-balanced wines which will age well. A good twin with the 1989 vintage.

Tuscany Perfect weather here too: intense heat, light rain to nourish and ripen the grapes, and cool evenings to conserve their acidity. Showers during early September helped produce healthy fruit, and here too grapes were brought in early. Even the late-ripening Sangiovese had been harvested by the end of September; the last reds were in by mid-October. Full, deeply-coloured, flavoury wines with round tannins and good acidity.

Whites ready to drink now. Chianti Classicos, which tend to be drunk too young, should be delicious from 1995 to well

*beyond 2000. Barolo and Barbaresco need bottle-age, the
former will be at its best between 2000 and 2010, and the best
Barolos 2010–20 or beyond.*

1989★ to ★★★★

The exceptionally good weather throughout much of Europe
was not experienced in Italy. Wet, often tempestuous conditions
characterised the summer and disastrous rain fell intermittently
during the harvest. This was the smallest vintage of the decade.

Piedmont Apart from a violent hailstorm in June which
damaged vines around Barolo (some growers lost as much as
60% of their crop), Piedmont largely escaped the bad weather.
Conditions were satisfactory and sound red and white grapes
were gathered. Overall, the yield was down by 15%. Perhaps the
best reds of the decade.

Tuscany A very mixed year. Some areas had too much rain
while others had too little and suffered drought. The Chianti was
better than the Chianti Classico and few *riservas* will be made.
Best wines came from Montalcino and Montepulciano. Overall,
light, early developers.

*Drink up the lighter dry whites. Barolo and Barbaresco
from 1999 to well after 2020. Chiantis, say, 1993–99.*

1988★★★★★

Generally, an excellent vintage for Italian wines. The yield,
however, was very small – Tuscany brought in its smallest crop
for 25 years.

Piedmont Cold, wet weather during the flowering resulted
in an incomplete flower set. Warm, damp weather followed,
encouraging the development of mildew in late June. Thereafter
the summer was hot and dry, aiding the development of ripe and
healthy grapes. However, rain during the harvest caused
problems, especially with the Nebbiolo and the later-picked
grapes in Barolo and Barbaresco. The Barbera, however, was
picked just before the rain and made wine of good quality.

Tuscany As in Piedmont, a cold start to the year impaired
the flower set, and yields were further reduced by severe heat
and drought. However, the harvest, which began on September
22 for the Cabernet grapes and October 1 for the Sangiovese,
produced high quality wines.

The *riservas* were fruity with high tannin levels; and the
best wines came from Montalcino where weather conditions had
been less severe. The harvest was early and the crop of above
average size.

*Whites all delicious now; drink up. It is a shame to drink the
great classic reds too soon: they need at least 10 years bottle-
age. To be realistic: Chiantis and the good* vini de tavola
*1995–2005, Barbaresco 2000–20, Barolo and Brunello di
Montalcino 2003–30.*

1987★★ to ★★★

A year of variable quality, somewhat overshadowed by the
superior 1988 vintage.

Piedmont A cold winter was followed by a cool but dry
spring. Conditions were generally fine throughout the summer,
with the exception of a rather cool July. August and September
saw some welcome light rain and the harvest began in early

October. The crop was of average size.

Tuscany The vines flowered under excellent conditions but their progress was then hampered by a long, dry spell which lasted from July until late September.

The harvest, which began on September 23 for Cabernet grapes and October 3 for the Sangiovese, took place in many areas during damp, rot-inducing weather. In Montalcino, however, the grapes were picked earlier on and a large quantity of excellent quality wines was produced.

Overall, these were light and enjoyable, though not likely candidates for *riserva* status.

Most whites should have been drunk. All but the very best reds drink now.

1986★★★★

A good year which provided better drinking than the '87s but fell into the shadow of the tiny but excellent crop produced during the 1985 vintage.

Piedmont The winter was unusually cold and the spring was wet. All of Italy sizzled under a heatwave during May which broke at the end of the month with unsettled weather and sometimes violent hailstorms. These were, however, very localised. Some growers lost their entire crop, while others escaped altogether. Sadly, some of the affected areas were the top sites, including Barolo where growers lost up to 40% of their crop. The rest of the summer was hot, dry and humid. Rain during the first ten days of September fleshed out the grapes which were then fully ripened by two weeks of hot weather. The harvest began during the last week of September and a small quantity of good quality grapes was picked. Forward wines for mid-term drinking.

Tuscany Here a large crop was harvested after a hot summer which, with the exception of the odd burst of rain in July, was mainly dry. Picking began on September 22. 1986 produced some good, fruity Chiantis but few *riservas*. The Brunello and Vino Nobile were of average quality and the top *vini da tavola* are now showing elegance.

Most reds are starting to drink well now.

1985★★★★★

An extremely good vintage throughout Italy but, perhaps even more importantly, the year in which a shift of attitudes was perceived and a new era of more serious winemaking began, particularly in Tuscany.

Piedmont An exceptionally cold winter gave way to a warm, dry spring. A rather uneven summer followed, yet superb wines were made, particularly by the best individual producers in the best districts. Those from Barolo were very successful, making deep-coloured, richly tannic, long-lasting wines.

Tuscany Even better than Piedmont. Similar weather conditions. Superb estate wines can be found, some full of fruit and ready for drinking, some tannic and needing bottle-age. They are worth buying and drinking.

Wonderful wines. Great depth of fruit. Mouthfilling without being coarse. The big Barbarescos, Barolos and Brunellos though delicious, are still infants. They will be at their best from 2000 to 2020, or beyond. Chiantis drinking well now but the top wines need more bottle-age, say 1995–2005.

1984★★

A poor year throughout Italy, with the possible exceptions of Sicily and Sardinia and northern Piedmont.

Piedmont Cold, wet weather in May and June led to a late and incomplete flowering. The weather was cool and unsettled throughout the summer and the grapes were not fully ripened in time for the harvest. The wines were thin and unripe.

Tuscany A similar story to Piedmont, with almost continuous September rain. Ironically, this was the year in which Chianti was promoted to DOCG status.

Drink up.

1983★★ to ★★★★

An uneven year: disappointing for some, excellent for others.

Piedmont The vines flowered during rain, July was hot and humid and some growers experienced problems with rot. Uneven weather in late summer improved in time for the harvest in October. The crop was of average size and the best growers, who selected their grapes rigorously, made very good wines. Elsewhere the quality was often poor.

Tuscany A good year. Spring was mild and the vines flowered in early June. Summer was fine with just the required amount of rain. In Chianti the weather continued unbroken until the harvest which began on September 22 – *riserva* Chiantis made delightful drinking. In Montalcino the weather deteriorated during harvest, and careful selection was needed.

Drink up, though the 'new wave' of Chiantis are still delightful and Barolos, as always, will keep longer.

1982★★★★

An excellent vintage throughout Tuscany and Piedmont.

Piedmont Mild, dry weather during the spring pushed growth ahead of normal. Some vineyards were damaged by hail in late April but overall there were few problems. Summer was hot and dry with some rain in late September/early October prior to the harvest. An average crop: rich, ripe, flavoury wines.

Tuscany A long, cold winter relented with a sudden change in the temperature in May. Apart from the odd wet period and hail in early September, the weather was hot and sunny, approaching drought conditions. Picking began on September 20 and the quality of the wine was consistently good for all of Tuscany. The top *riservas* were outstanding.

A most attractive year. Highly regarded Sassicaia excellent, with life in hand. Classic Barolos still laden with tannin.

1981★★★

An uneven and generally disappointing year.

Piedmont Winter was long and cold. Vines then suffered rot during a hot, humid June and July. Apart from a wet patch in late August/early September the weather was cloudy but dry until the harvest, beginning in late September. Careful selection of grapes was essential. The best wines were the Barbarescos.

Tuscany Overall, a much better year for this part of Italy. Spring was late but hot and the good weather continued almost without interruption through the summer. The harvest, beginning on September 20, was staggered thanks to rain midway. Consequently the wines made from grapes picked before the rain are of superior quality to those made later. They were elegant with good ageing potential.

Some very rich wines but overall variable. Drink up.

1980★

A moderate year, although inevitably there were good, if not outstanding exceptions.

Piedmont A mild winter ran into a cool spring which lasted until June. Growth was retarded until July when the weather suddenly became hot and dry. These conditions lasted until late September when rain fell until early October. The harvest started extremely late and was interrupted by snow on November 4. An average sized crop was picked.

Tuscany Tuscany saw very similar weather conditions to Piedmont. Picking started in early October but was delayed by rain and many growers found that they did not finish until November. On the whole the grapes were ripe and healthy and some very good wines were made.

Drink up.

1979★★★★

Piedmont Nearly equal in size to 1980 but of better quality. Very good early-maturing wines from Barolo and Barbaresco, while further north the wines were well-structured, with better-than-average life expectancy.

Tuscany Here too a huge harvest of good to very good quality: particularly the Montepulciano and Brunello di Montalcino; not, however, for long keeping.

Chiantis at peak now. Can still be superb. The great producers' Barolos are magnificent and will age further. Sassicaia perfection yet will keep another 5–10 years.

1978★★★★★

The best all-round vintage of the 1970s.

Piedmont Damp, cold weather in spring and early summer brought the vintage near to disaster. A warm, dry autumn saved the day: small crops of fine Barolo and Barbaresco, for ageing.

Tuscany Similar conditions to those in Piedmont produced a small vintage with some outstanding, long-lived wines, especially the Brunello, Carmignano and Chianti Classico.

Superb reds, the best perfection now yet with time in hand.

1977★ to ★★★

Piedmont Not a good year: small crop, generally poor wine.

Tuscany A warm spring and dry summer made some very good Brunellos, Vino Nobiles and some good Chiantis.

Drink up.

1976★

Piedmont A vintage of uneven quality in Asti/Alba but a fine harvest in Novarra-Vercelli; the Gattinara was excellent, others were sturdy wines to be drunk quickly.

Tuscany A disastrous year: wet spring and summer weather. *Drink up.*

1975★ to ★★★

Piedmont A mediocre year, yet some delightful wines.

Tuscany A fair year. A rainy spring followed by a very dry, sometimes stormy summer. Particularly good for Brunello, Vino Nobile and Chianti from the Siena area.

Even the best reds fully mature. Drink up.

1974★★ to ★★★★

Piedmont An excellent, abundant vintage for long keeping.

Tuscany Except for some excellent Chianti Rufina, a poor, unreliable year.

Only the substantial reds, Barbaresco, Barolo and the top Brunello worth looking out for. Drink up.

1973★★★

Piedmont An uneven year, mostly only fair but some excellent wines from Ghemme.

Tuscany Similar to Piedmont, with some excellent wines from Carmignano.

Fully mature. Drink up.

1972

Piedmont A disaster: both Barolo and Barbaresco were declassified as DOC. Further north the wines were fair to good but only ever short-lived.

Tuscany Again, a poor year with wet weather through spring and summer. The exception was Sassicaia.

Generally avoid.

1971★★★★★

Piedmont For Barolo and Barbaresco this was possibly the best year since the war.

Tuscany Overall, a very good though uneven vintage. The best wines were from Chianti, some disappointments in Montalcino and Montepulciano.

The better Barolos and Barbarescos at peak but will continue; Brunello has more to come. Top Chianti Classicos are perfect now though some on decline. The 'new reds', Sassicaia, Tignanello, Rubesco Torgiano all superb, fully mature.

1970★★★

Piedmont A large sized crop of excellent wines, standing somewhat in the shadow of the '71s, sometimes unfairly.

Tuscany A good year: excellent Brunello and Vino Nobile.

Fully mature. Only the top Barolos have time in hand. The rest, drink up.

OTHER OUTSTANDING VINTAGES

Piedmont Barolo: **1964, 1961, 1958, 1952. Tuscany** Brunello: **1967, 1964, 1961, 1955, 1945.** Chianti: **1968, 1967, 1964, 1962, 1957, 1947.** Vino Nobile: **1967, 1958.**

SPAIN

FOR OVER A CENTURY AND A HALF SHERRY WAS
the quality wine of Spain, table wines being indifferent to
execrable, or if good, relatively unknown. The dramatic upturn
began in Rioja in the 1960s, and a decade later one family in
Penedès, Torres, experimenting – as they still are – with
different grape varieties grown at different altitudes, and superb
winemaking and marketing, carved a niche which has raised the
whole conception of what Spain can produce commercially.

La Mancha, to the south of Madrid, still produces 50 percent
of Spain's total production of table wines. But wines from this
area, and nearby Valdepeñas, are not in the same league as those
from Penedès, Rioja, neighbouring Navarra, and the two odd-
men out from the Ribera del Duero east of Valladolid: a relative
newcomer, Pesquera, and Spain's only long-established, classic
(highly priced) red wine, Vega Sicilia. It needs to be stated that
Vega Sicilia spends up to ten years in wood, so, for drinking
dates, one must add at least 12 years to the vintage.

The white wines of Spain, sherry excepted, were once
uniformly atrocious, but tend now to range from passable to
good though few are exceptional and hardly any, in my opinion,
warrant cellaring for more than a year or two. The following
vintages notes refer mostly, therefore, to the better quality red
wines. The latter have the added advantage of still being very
reasonably priced for their quality. Really old vintages,
particularly of Rioja, can occasionally be found. They seem
either cheap for their age or wildly overpriced, but in either case
are rarely more than interesting.

1991★★★★

Variable but mainly very good quality, production in general
down 20% from 1990 but of approximately the five-year
average level.

Rioja Autumn rain, wind and cold weather merely delayed a
week or so the picking of fully ripe grapes.

Penedès Severe spring frosts caused worrying losses but
from then on weather conditions were well-nigh perfect. The
final crop here was around 30–40%, half that originally feared,
but of extremely high quality. All grape varieties were picked in
perfect conditions.

Ribera del Duero The quality was good but quantity down.

The only real disaster was in Jerez where 'industrial action',
a prolonged strike, resulted in much acrimony and loss of grapes
for the production of sherry.

1990★★★★

After two years of troublesome weather conditions, Spain
enjoyed a dry but relatively normal year and produced, in many
instances, some excellent wines.

Rioja A very dry winter was followed by an exceptionally
hot summer and a harvest which began two weeks ahead of
normal. The sizzling heat affected mainly the lower areas of the
Rioja, while Tempranillo grapes from the higher slopes were of
excellent quality, benefiting from the cooler, moister summer
nights. Disease was not a problem at all this year. Late
refreshing rains were an advantage but the extreme heat may
mean that the wines have less body than those of the previous

year. Overall, the reds should be better than the whites, which are rather low in acidity.

Penedès The summer here was not excessively hot, and cool nights and rains during June and July were beneficial. The main harvest began mid-September and the white grape harvest was large. In the Alt Penedès a few very violent hailstorms possibly affected the finest white grapes but not the overall volume, which was higher than usual. Torres predicted this to be a great year for his Milmanda Chardonnay: a spring frost had reduced yields, concentrating sugars and consequently increasing the potential alcohol levels of these wines. The same can also be said for the Merlot, Sauvignon Blanc, Pinot Noir and Cabernet Sauvignon.

Ribera del Duero Despite a very dry summer yields here were up by more than 35%: good news after the two previous years, particularly as this is likely to be a very good year.

Most Riojas will make pleasant early drinking, the Duero reds will be excellent: Pesquera doubtless on best form around 1995–2000, whilst Vega Sicilia, as mentioned in the introduction, will have a longer life span, probably being marketed in 2002 and reaching its zenith around 2020. Most dry white wines are best drunk now; only the scarcer Chardonnays and the like, better with a little bottle-age.

1989★★★

After the appalling difficulties faced the previous year, the main problem for growers this year was the drought, which cut the total yield in Spain by 11%.

Rioja Despite drought conditions, the harvest was reasonably bountiful. A slightly better vintage for the reds than the whites, which tended to be high in alcohol and low in fruit. The reds are well-structured and the best will be the *crianzas* and the *reservas*. The whites are rather heavy.

Penedès Good conditions throughout the summer were spoiled by two hailstorms, the first in late August and the second in early September, which reduced the size of the harvest considerably. As with Rioja, this was a better year for the reds than the whites.

Ribera del Duero Dry weather reduced yields here by around 20%. The quality, however, was excellent.

Reds now–1998, the exception, as always, being Vega Sicilia which will not be put on the market for another decade. Whites, drink up.

1988 at best ★★★

Spain experienced more than its fair share of disastrous weather this year. The wettest spring on record was followed by a poor summer. This was made worse by the development of rot on the vines, a rare situation for which Spanish growers were unprepared. Widespread heavy hailstorms then followed.

To an extent, the quality wine regions of Spain escaped the worst effects of the weather, partly thanks to better success at mastering the problems.

Rioja A wet start to the year resulted in a late flowering and uneven fruit set, but this was compensated for by excellent picking conditions (October 24 to November 2). A fair size crop was harvested and the quality was very satisfactory.

Penedès The growers who controlled the spread of mildew

most successfully, produced the best wines. Harvest began on September 10 and continued in the high Penedès into the second half of October. There was some rainfall during picking but cool temperatures and dry soil prevented the spread of *Botrytis*. Some very good wines.

Ribera del Duero Rain, hail and mildew reduced the crop by 50%; some desperate growers requested that this area be declared a disaster zone.

Reds of better producers drinking well now and will keep.

1987★★★ to ★★★★★

Rioja A very good year. The mild winter and hot, dry spring resulted in an early flowering. A cool, period followed, with some slight frost in May, but summer arrived rapidly and held out for the harvest which lasted from October 14 to 23.

Penedès As with Rioja, favourable weather conditions made this an excellent year. After an exceptionally hot summer the harvest began during the third week of August for the Muscat and continued until the end of October for the Parellada grapes. Here, heavy rains during the late harvest resulted in the development of *Botrytis* on the broken grape skins. Damage, however, was minimal and the Parellada grapes produced pleasant, if light, wines.

Miguel Torres declared that this was his best vintage in 15 years for red wines, especially those from Cabernet Sauvignon, with deep colour, excellent tannin, and good ageing potential.

Ribera del Duero A mild winter and wet spring was followed by exceptionally hot weather from May until August, which caused the grapes to overripen in some areas. September rain caused rot and diluted the level of acidity in the grapes. The quantity was high for this vintage but the quality was variable, ranging from average to no more than good.

Riojas, now–1997; the Cabernet Sauvignon from Penedès say from now to beyond 2000; all other reds drink soon.

1986★ to ★★★

A successful year throughout much of Spain, although weather conditions caused problems in Penedès.

Rioja Spring was late after a cold, dry winter, delaying bud-break and flowering. Warm, dry weather continued throughout the summer, broken only by rain in April and October. Harvest took place from October 20–28 in good conditions and the crop was below average size. The wines have good ageing potential.

Penedès The initial problem in this region was the drought which continued from May until August. When the rain did eventually fall it swelled the sun-dried grapes, causing the skins to split and the rapid spread of *Botrytis*. Growers were therefore forced to pick quickly and selectively. Torres reported that his Cabernet Sauvignon and Tempranillo had been severely affected by the rot, causing him to reject 40% of the latter. However, where the grapes had been picked early, the wines were of better quality.

All to be drunk soon.

1985★★★★

One of the driest years for some time in Spain, although a few areas, including Rioja, suffered less from drought than others.

Rioja The drought started during a cold, dry winter and continued throughout a good flowering, an extremely hot summer, and held through the harvest which started October 20. Fortunately, the soil had retained much of the moisture from the previous wet autumn and so the region harvested a huge crop and made many very good, tannic, long-lasting wines. The best came from the high areas.

Penedès Conversely, the drought did reduce yields in this region. However, the growing season was cooler with warm days and cool nights. This was a small vintage of healthy grapes with good sugar levels which produced very good wines, especially the reds.

Ribera del Duero Classified as a 'good' year.

Even the most tannic reds are softening and drinking well. Possibly at best 1995–99.

1984★★

The end of a four-year drought in Spain.

Rioja A mild, humid winter, frost in May, hail in September, and the appearance of hurricane Hortensia in October, all made this a problematic year. The yield was consequently small and the wines of average quality – not suitable for long keeping.

Penedès Flowering took place successfully after a fine spring. Growth was retarded by the mild, damp conditions which prevailed throughout the summer and the harvest started late in October. A good vintage; Miguel Torres noted this as a year for white wines, the reds have also shown much promise.

Ribera del Duero Classified as an 'average' year.

All should be drunk by now, with the possible exception of Torres' top reds.

1983★★★

Despite weather problems a passably good year for Spanish wines, though standing very much in the shadow of its two predecessors.

Rioja Cold winter, heavy frost in early spring, hail in May around Nájera, Cenicero and Lapuebla and very hot weather during the harvest, all of which conspired to damage crops. Uneven quality: some disappointments yet some very promising wines with good colour.

Penedès A cold, snowy winter was followed by a hot spring. A summer-long drought – the worst for 150 years – broke in September. Thereafter the grapes ripened perfectly and the harvest began during the first week of October. Both the reds and the whites were good, fruity wines.

Drink up.

1982★★★★★

As with Bordeaux, this was an outstanding year which many felt would rank alongside the classic vintages of the century.

Rioja A warm, dry winter was followed by a hot, dry spring. Drought conditions prevailed, causing a loss of around 20% of the yield, but some much-needed rain arrived in August. The harvest ran from October 22 until November 3.

These are wines with great ageing potential; many, especially the *gran reservas*, will reward long keeping.

Penedès A wet spring was followed by a very hot summer – July was the hottest for 100 years – caused by hot winds blowing off the Sahara. The hot weather eventually broke and harvesting began during the first week of October. Impressive wines which, again, have good potential.

Ribera del Duero Classified as 'excellent'.

Certainly one of the rare vintages to provide red wines which will not only keep but benefit from long cellaring – well into the 21st century.

1981★★ to ★★★★

Rioja A long, cold, frosty winter, with snow in April, eventually gave way to warmer weather. Flowering was early and thereafter hot, dry weather held throughout the summer until the abundant harvest at the end of October.

The wines were officially classified as 'good' and thought by some to be excellent. For the wines of Navarra this was undoubtedly the vintage of the decade.

Penedès Flowering was delayed by a cold, showery spring. Conditions improved later with a warm, dry summer during which gentle, beneficial rain fell in mid-June and late July. An early harvest started in the last two weeks of September. Small crop of good wines – some were classified as excellent – but they are mainly past their best.

Drink up.

1980★★★

Rioja A mild, wet, frostless spring was followed by a cool but humid summer. The harvest, which ran from October 5 to November 12, took place during very cold but sunny weather and yielded a large crop. This was an elegant vintage, classified as 'good' by the Consejo, but the wines tended to lack body and were not for long keeping.

Penedès A long, wet spring delayed the flowering which, despite heavy rain, was successful. Temperatures were moderate throughout the very dry summer but rose in August and the weather remained fine for the harvest. A successful year for Torres' wines, particularly the reds.

Riojas should have been drunk. Top Penedès reds are mature.

1979★

Rioja A mild, wet winter was followed by an early, frostless spring and fine summer. Hopes for an excellent vintage were dashed by heavy pre-harvest rain which caused rot. A large crop of average quality wines.

Penedès After a wet spring the vines blossomed and matured well. Hot summer weather continued until the end of August when light rains fell. September was initially wet but warm and harvest was completed during a very rainy October. This year had shown promise but the quality was affected by the summer drought and autumn rain. Average sized crop of average quality.

Few to be seen. Drink up.

1978★★★

Rioja Wet winter weather continued into the spring. Severe night frosts affecting flowering, consequently reducing the potential crop; however, conditions improved, with a dry, sunny summer and autumn. The harvest, which took place from October 20 to 30, produced well-balanced, fruity wines which have aged excellently.

Penedès A wet, fresh spring was followed by a mild but dry and sunny summer. There was some light, timely rain in early September and the harvest began at the end of the month in warm, dry weather. A below average crop of good wines.

Worth looking out for. Reds now fully mature and the best are drinking well.

1977★ to ★★

Rioja A year of difficult weather conditions. Persistent, although not intense, spring frosts were followed by heavy rains and a very cool summer. The autumn was mild but this was not enough to save the vintage. Mediocre wines.

Penedès Also a cool summer but, fortunately, warm, sunny weather during September and October enabled the grapes to ripen well, resulting in very satisfactory wines; the best made very exciting drinking.

Now well past best.

1976★★

Rioja A variable year. Winter cold and dry, budding delayed by a very cold March, summer was hot and wet. Consequently the vines matured unevenly and the wines were very variable.

Penedès A cool, wet spring followed by a warm, sunny summer moderated by some timely storms. But good wines.

Drink up.

1975★★★★

Rioja A very dry winter delayed budding. Spring was wet, followed by a hot summer which continued into the harvest. Many of the white grapes developed *Botrytis*. On the whole this was a very good vintage for the red wines which had good ageing potential.

Penedès The weather conditions proved ideal. Warm, sunny days throughout the summer with the occasional shower early-on. The grapes ripened beautifully and picking began in early October.

Fully mature and the best still drinking well.

1974★

Rioja A damp, very cold winter was followed by heavy rains at the beginning of spring. Summer was hot and dry. A mediocre vintage.

Penedès Moderately good.

Drink up.

1973★★★

Rioja Winter was cold and dry followed by a mild, dry, frostless spring. Summer was hot with only the occasional shower, leading to a warm autumn. Generally a good year.

Penedès A mild, cool spring preceded a dry, sunny summer.

Grapes were freshened by light pre-harvest rain. Picking began early September.

Ribera del Duero (Vega Sicilia) A short vegetative cycle, late blossoming, and a summer of hot days and cool nights. Good harvest.

Pleasant wines now past their best except for the rare Vega Sicilia, drinking beautifully.

1972

Rioja The second of two poor years in Rioja. A very cold winter delayed budding and conditions did not improve with a cool, wet spring and summer. Growers experienced great problems with oidium.

Penedès Not a good year.

Avoid.

1971

Rioja A very wet spring followed a cold, dry winter. Late frosts in May and wet weather throughout the spring resulted in widespread attacks of oidium which greatly reduced the size of the crop. Thereafter the weather was hot and dry. A poor year.

Penedès Excellent.

Fully mature now.

1970★★★★ to ★★★★★

Rioja A cold, wet winter delayed budding and some vines were damaged by hail in June, but otherwise a warm, moist summer and a moderate autumn. Very good wines.

Penedès A legendary year in this region which provided ideal conditions for red winemaking. The crop was small but the quality excellent. The 1970 Torres Gran Coronas Black Label came top in the Cabernet Sauvignon class at the 1979 Gault Millau 'Wine Olympics', beating even the Latour and La Mission-Haut-Brion.

The best, particularly the Torres Gran Coronas Black label, still lovely.

EARLIER VINTAGES

Rioja The following were all regarded as excellent years: **1968, 1964, 1962, 1959, 1955, 1952, 1948, 1947, 1942, 1924, 1922, 1920, 1906, 1898, 1897** and **1894**.

Penedès Excellent years: **1964, 1958, 1955, 1952, 1934, 1924, 1922.** Very good years: **1968, 1963, 1959, 1954, 1949, 1948, 1947, 1942, 1935, 1931, 1928, 1925.**

Vega Sicilia (from recent tasting notes) Excellent: **1966, 1964, 1960, 1957, 1953** Good years: **1969, 1965, 1962, 1948, 1942.**

PORTUGUESE TABLE WINE

VINTAGES MATTER IN PORTUGAL MORE THAN MOST people seem to realise. There are few catastrophic years but, in spite of the warm climate, there are considerable variations between different harvests. This is especially true in the north of the country where the best years for table wine often correspond closely to 'declared' port vintages. In the newer wine producing regions of southern Portugal, excessive heat and drought is often a problem. But, with modern equipment in their *adegas*, winemakers are now learning to make the best use of these extreme conditions.

Most of the Portuguese wines currently on sale come from vintages since the mid-1980s. The two principal exceptions are: Barca Velha from port producers Ferreira, and Buçaco from the unique Palace Hotel deep in the heart of the country, both of which reward long keeping. The cellars at the Buçaco Palace house wines dating back to the 1940s and even older bottles occasionally turn up for auction.

There are other well-made reds which keep well, notably those from Bucelas and the Dão and Bairrada districts: some of the best can be found dating back to the 1960s. On the other hand, matured ('maduro') white wines are something of an acquired taste, but with improvements in vinification a number are becoming more acceptably international in style.

Most Vinho Verde is labelled without a vintage date. These wines should always be drunk while young and fresh. Varietal Vinhos Verdes, however, made exclusively from the Alvarinho grape, are usually from a specified year and may benefit from maturing in bottle. The Palacio de Brejoeira makes one of the finest examples.

One thing all Portugal's wines have in common is good value.

1991★★ to ★★★★

After a wet winter, warm weather in April and May bought on early growth. June was unusually cool and wet but this was more than compensated for by hot weather which lasted uninterrupted until the end of August. In the north, a large crop looked likely, however, rain in early September led to rot. Some Vinho Verde growers lost 15% of their crop. In the south, three weeks of extreme heat undoubtedly caused a set back and, for the third successive year, a lack of water kept yields down below average.

With financial help from the European Community, wineries all over Portugal are becoming even better equipped to cope with climatic extremes. Although most producers seem pleased with the quality of their wine, some southern reds (especially those made in the old-fashioned *adegas* where temperature control is lacking) tend to be unbalanced and over alcoholic.

Vinho Verde drinking now; other whites over the next 18 months. Middle quality reds 1994–97, high quality reds 1995–2002.

1990★★★

Heavy winter rains around Christmas 1989 replenished the water-table in much of the country, but a prolonged period of dry summer weather, combined with searing heat, quickly brought on a drought in some regions.

Yields were down by about 10% in Alentejo and on the Setúbal Peninsula, though this was more than compensated for by some high quality wines. In the north, two short bursts of rain in August and September helped to swell the grapes. Growers in Bairrada, Dão and the Douro harvested an average sized crop of well-ripened grapes.

Vinho Verde should have been drunk; other whites drinking soon. The middle quality reds now–1996; sturdiest reds 1994–98.

1989★★★

As in so much of Europe, July and August were blisteringly hot throughout Portugal. After the previous year's extremely low yield, a large crop was badly needed. In the event, drought in some parts of Portugal retarded development of the grapes, and overall reduced average yields by as much as 20%.

The early harvest produced ripe fruit, though some wines suffer from a lack of acidity. In Bairrada they tend to lack colour and depth.

Drink up the white wines. Red wines should be drunk soon, particularly the southern reds which are drinking very well now.

1988★★★★

Disasters are not frequent in Portugal's mild Atlantic climate, but in 1988 vineyards in much of the country came close to catastrophe.

An uneven flowering was followed by rain which continued until the end of June. Many small growers in the north had never experienced such conditions before and mildew set in before anything could be done to prevent it. The Minho was particularly badly hit; yields were in some cases 80% below the average.

Low yields often mean high quality and the 1988 vintage was saved by a warm, dry summer which lasted until the end of the harvest.

Outstanding wines were made in Dão, Bairrada and the Alentejo. In the Douro, which suffered the effects of the poor spring, most of the production was used to make port.

Drink up whites. Reds are long-lasting.

1987★ to ★★

An uneven year. In the north, high temperatures during early summer brought on a drought which slowed down the maturation of the grapes. Consequently, many wines from Bairrada, Dão and Setúbal were light, astringent and somewhat lacking in colour. The best wines were produced further south in the Alentejo.

Drink up whites and northern reds. Southern reds drinking well now and for the next 3 years.

1986★★★

For many winemakers in the north 1986 was a year to forget. A warm summer was followed by torrential rain at the time of the harvest. Rot set in quickly, badly affecting vineyards in Bairrada, Dão and parts of the Douro.

The south fared better; some excellent, well-structured wines were produced in the Alentejo and on the Setúbal Peninsula.

Most need drinking up. Well-structured Alentejo reds now drinking well.

1985★★★★

In many ways, the reverse of 1986. After a wet spring, the late hot summer and warm sunny autumn ripened the grapes and provided perfect harvesting conditions.

The Dão, Bairrada and the Douro in the north of the country produced intense, concentrated wines which have the potential to mature well.

In the south, however, the piercing sun shrivelled grapes in many of the vineyards before they were picked. High temperatures caused problems during fermentation in the less well-equipped *adegas*, and many of the resulting wines suffered from excess acidity.

Top reds from the north and southern garrafeiras have excellent fruit and are well-balanced; they are lovely now and will keep.

1984★★★

Rain in early October followed a cool summer and many growers were caught short waiting for their grapes to ripen. As a result, Dão and Bairrada made thin, astringent red wines; the best came from the Douro.

Further south, vines benefited from a relatively cool vintage and good, well-balanced reds were made in the Alentejo and Setúbal regions.

All now fully mature.

1983★★★★★

The second of two excellent vintages. Good weather throughout the spring and summer months ensured a crop of ripe, healthy fruit. However, some winemakers found fermentation difficult in the increasingly hot weather.

Overall, the north produced classic, firm-flavoured reds. To the south, where the use of modern equipment is less common, the wines were somewhat less balanced, many having stewed aromas and flavours.

Drink up all but the top quality reds which have a 10–15 year life span.

1982★★★★★

After hot summer conditions growers harvested early.

The Douro, Dão and Bairrada regions made robust wines with plenty of ripe fruit. Ferreira's Barca Velha has a chocolatey intensity and Buçaco produced some intensely ripe and full-flavoured reds.

Further south, 1982 had the edge on the 1983 vintage; particularly in the Ribatejo, where some excellent, ripe *garrafeiras* were made.

Now to 1996.

1981★

A year which many growers would prefer to forget. A cold spring retarded growth, and rain in September encouraged rot. Picking began late.

The wines were often thin and astringent, lacking fruit and depth. The eastern Douro escaped the worst of the rain and produced a good spicy Barca Velha from Ferreira – the high note of the year.

Drink up.

1980★★★★★

For many winemakers throughout Portugal this was the best vintage of the decade. A late flowering was followed by a warm summer and a dry autumn, and the grapes were harvested in perfect condition.

The Dão and Bairrada regions made fruity, well-balanced wines and further south in the Ribatejo some excellent *garrafeiras* were produced. Curiously, Ferreira did not make a Barca Velha in this year, preferring to declassify its wine as Reserva Especial.

Fully mature now but the best reds will keep.

EARLIER VINTAGES

Notable earlier vintages include: **1978, 1975, 1974, 1971, 1970, 1966. Barca Velha: 1978, 1966, 1965, 1964. Buçaco: 1978, 1977, 1975, 1970, 1966, 1965, 1962** and, particularly, **1959.**

CALIFORNIA

IT IS ROUGHLY 700 MILES FROM THE MOST southerly vineyards of California, near San Diego, to Mendocino in the north; and in terms of average temperature, the range varies considerably between the near coastal districts and the broad, hot Central Valley. It is therefore not practicable to include weather reports and quality assessments for such widely differing areas. Similarly it is no reflection on the quality of wine made in around Santa Barbara, Monterey or Santa Clara if the following vintage notes concentrate solely on the two major, now classic, wine districts: the Napa Valley, with its almost continuous and contiguous string of premium quality vineyards and wineries, and the broader, equally vine-clad, Sonoma County.

If we take into account the vines planted by Spanish missionaries, the history of wine in what is now California, though not as ancient as that of the Cape, predates all other 'New World' wine cultures. The business of vine growing was revived in the second half of the 19th century and, after the blight of Prohibition, took off again seriously in the 1940s, gaining momentum in the 1950s, making tremendous strides in the 1970s and climaxing, both in terms of volume and quality, in the 1980s.

Virtually every variety of *Vitis vinifera* has been cultivated in California, but, by process of elimination, Cabernet Sauvignon and Chardonnay stand supreme. Zinfandel ploughs its lonely furrow, Sauvignon Blanc (Fumé Blanc) fills an important niche, Pinot Noir is achieving distinction, and the once dull Johannisberg Riesling has found its apotheosis in late-harvest dessert wines.

Like most light dry white wine, Sauvignon Blanc is best drunk young – indeed it does not age at all well. However, the best Chardonnay, pleasant drinking at three years of age, can be consumed with equal enjoyment some eight years after the vintage. The best reds, like Bordeaux and burgundy, need bottle-age though California Cabernets and 'Zins' have an innate flesh and fruitiness which enables them to be drunk when 'released' (put on the market) by the producer. Those of high quality, with a track record, and from a good vintage, can develop well for 20 years or longer. California has certainly come of age.

1991 ★★★★★

A worrying year which ended satisfactorily. Weather conditions were similar in the Napa Valley and Sonoma County: record low temperatures in the winter and an ominously dry New Year and early spring. Happily, before bud-break in March, there was exceptionally heavy rain. The spring was cool but the flowering successful, promising an abundant crop. However, the summer was also cool, by California standards, and extended. Leaves were removed to enable the sun to penetrate, and crops thinned to encourage concentration and maturation, the latter finally brought to a conclusion by an excellent unbroken Indian summer. Ripe grapes with good levels of acidity were brought in before late October rains.

The long cool growing season resulted in good natural levels of acidity – vital for life and balance – levels of alcohol conducive to finesse rather than massive structure, yet with enhanced concentration and flavour for all varietals and intensity of colour for the reds. The only cloud on the horizon, particularly in the Napa, is the spread of phylloxera (Type B) which is devastating whole blocks of vines on the valley floor, necessitating extensive and expensive replanting. There are good reasons therefore, for keeping track – and buying – wines of this potentially excellent vintage.

Some of the fresh, acidic Sauvignon Blancs will be delightful to drink now; Chardonnays perhaps now–1998, depending on their weight and quality; Pinot Noirs 1994–99, and Cabernet Sauvignons and related blends drinking from 1995 to well beyond 2000.

1990★★★★

A smaller crop than the previous year's, but one which was harvested in near-perfect conditions, particularly in the Napa Valley, promising an excellent year for California wines.

Napa Valley Another dry winter, with below average temperatures, led to a late bud-break. However, a long heatwave in mid-May speeded growth up. Flowering and berry set were affected by heavy rains in late May, resulting in a smaller than average crop. Picking began early (mid-August); cool mornings and evenings with gradual warming during the days characterised the harvest, making this, some say, one of the most ideal in recent history.

Overall, the grapes were in good condition; fruit was mature and acid and sugar levels were well-balanced to give intense, characterful red wines and rich whites.

Sonoma County Normal bud break, followed by moderate weather, led to a good set in the Chardonnay grapes, but the Cabernet and Sauvignon Blanc did not set well due to heavy rain in June. Thereafter the summer was fine, interrupted by short two-day heatwaves.

Harvesting proceeded normally in near-perfect conditions, with many Sauvignon Blancs being picked early at the same time as the Chardonnay. As with the Napa Valley, small yields of high quality, intense, deep-coloured wines.

Sauvignon Blancs ready now. Chardonnays now to, say, 1998; classic reds 1994–2000.

1989★★★ to ★★★★

A year which will be remembered for the devastating earthquake which struck in mid-October, causing thousands of bottles of the previous vintage to be shattered.

Napa Valley After several drought years, rain in March was much welcomed by growers in California. The vines flowered in ideal conditions which held throughout the summer, encouraging high expectations for this vintage. However, towards the end of September, with 40% of the grapes picked, the harvest was interrupted by widespread, torrential rain. Thereafter the weather was cold, foggy and stormy, encouraging the spread of rot on the remaining white grapes. Picking resumed later, those who picked quickly and selectively produced the best wines.

Yields were considerably larger than those of the previous dry years. Quality, however, was low.

Sonoma County Similar conditions prevailed here. However, near-perfect harvesting conditions produced some good wines. The Cabernet Sauvignon was deep-coloured with good, tannic structure.

Whites all drinking well. The best reds need considerable bottle-age.

1988★★★ to ★★★★

Described as one of the weirdest years on record because of the unusual weather conditions.

Napa Valley A dry winter and hot February and March encouraged early bud-break. Cold, rainy weather in April continued through the flowering, accompanied by heavy winds. The summer was exceptionally hot and harvesting began on August 24.

The drought and erratic weather conditions affected berry and bunch size, massively reducing the size of the crop. Growers reported that the tonnage of Pinot Noir was down by as much as 60% and the Sauvignon Blanc by 50%. Quality, however, was high and the best, made from grapes picked early and selectively, were good, concentrated wines.

Sonoma County Bud-break was delayed by a dry winter but growth caught up during a warm spring and the vines flowered in early April. Summer was initially cold and wet, and thereafter the growing season was alternately very hot or very cool.

The vintage was early: picking began in late August and, as with the Napa Valley, yields were low and quality high. Some finely-flavoured, well-balanced Chardonnays and Sauvignon Blancs resulted.

Sauvignon Blancs, drink up. Chardonnays mainly ready now but the best will keep a little longer. Pinot Noir now–1996; Cabernet and Cabernet blends now–1998.

1987★★★★

A small crop, but the grapes were very healthy and showed great potential.

Napa Valley Soils, made dry by low rainfall at the end of the previous season, produced vines with small berry and cluster size: factors which promised an excellent vintage. The growing season enjoyed fine, warm weather and the arrival of coastal fog cooled the grapes and protected acidity levels.

Picking was early: grapes for sparkling wines were picked in late July and the harvest was fully under way for all grapes by mid-August.

The white wines combined a good balance of acidity with high sugar levels and the red wines were of exceptional quality.

Sonoma County Warm, dry weather held throughout the winter and spring and flowering took place early during hot weather. High temperatures in May caused some berry shatter, especially in the Cabernet Sauvignon, and a consequent drop in the yield. Thereafter the weather was generally cool and dry and the harvest took place early in mid-August.

These are flavoury wines, though slightly less ripe than the '86s and '88s. A fine Cabernet Sauvignon vintage.

Whites, drink up. Cabernet Sauvignon, now–1998.

1986★★ to ★★★

Napa Valley A cold, dry winter ended with torrential storms in mid-February. Flowering was early but protracted, and the summer was dry and one of the coolest on record, but followed by hot weather in August and September.

The main harvest began early, around the beginning of September, but continued into October. Soft, round wines.

Sonoma County Despite heavy storms in February and a mild summer, the quality of the grapes by early September in the Russian River Valley was very good, with perfectly balanced sugar levels and acidity. Rains from mid- to late-September encouraged the development of rot among the last grapes to be picked. Otherwise, yields were high and the grapes had good tannin levels. Some excellent Cabernets.

Pinot Noirs drink now, Merlots now–1996, the better Cabernet Sauvignons now–1998.

1985★★★★★

Napa Valley Undoubtedly an excellent vintage – one of the best ever in this region.

Apart from some stormy weather in February, the weather was fine throughout the early spring and the summer. September saw some heavy rains which interrupted the main harvest, but good weather returned at the end of the month to ripen the remaining grapes.

A broad range of superbly balanced, supple, well-knit wines with excellent ageing potential.

Sonoma County A wet winter and early spring resulted in early bud-break. Apart from a few hot spells in June and July, the summer was mainly cool. The grapes ripened slowly and evenly, developing good concentration of fruit. Picking began around September 17, but the Cabernet harvest was interrupted in some areas by heavy rains. A small crop of good quality wines; promising Cabernets.

Whites should have been consumed by now. Pinot Noirs probably peaking, but the Cabernet Sauvignons drinking well, the best will continue to develop up to and even beyond 2000.

1984★★★

Napa Valley A very wet winter was followed by hot weather throughout the growing season. The summer was exceptionally hot – temperatures, sometimes well above 38°C (100°F), caused some berry shatter and consequently a reduction in the size of the crop.

The harvest was the earliest ever in the Napa region, all the major varietals ripening together, making picking extremely busy from as early as the first week of August. Clean grapes which made well-balanced, good quality wines with potential for ageing, although not quite up to the standard of the '85s.

Sonoma County As with the Napa Valley, a short season producing small berries and a smaller than average yield. Both the Chardonnay and Cabernet had good, fruity, aromatic flavours, but less finesse than the wines of cooler years. Overall, these were attractive wines for early drinking.

More of a Pinot Noir than Cabernet year, though reports conflict. Most whites now too old.

1983★ to ★★★

Napa Valley The wettest winter on record ran into a summer which, apart from one heatwave in mid-July, was damp and cool. These conditions caused considerable problems, including a lack of soil aeration and visibly 'tired', soggy vines, as well as the inevitable rot. The best-drained sites experienced the least problems and everywhere picking was very selective.

The harvest yielded a small crop of very variable wines which ranged from poor to excellent in quality. The best were the Cabernets.

Sonoma County Here too the year was characterised by excessive rainfall, followed by one of the coolest summers on record. Picking did not begin until mid-September and was also very selective. The final yield was the lowest of the decade.

Widespread *Botrytis* helped to produce some excellent Rieslings plus some equally good Gewurztraminers and late-harvest style Sauvignon Blancs. By contrast, this was not a good year for the Cabernets.

A distinctly uneven vintage, some reds very tannic, some soft. Hard to generalise. Best to drink up or avoid – except for the few good late-harvest wines at peak now.

1982 at best ★★★★

Napa Valley California suffered one of its wettest winters ever, followed by a frostless spring and good weather during flowering, providing ideal conditions for a bumper crop. Mid-September rains delayed the harvest for many Cabernets and some white grapes were lost to rot, although some very good *Botrytis* wines were made.

Overall, this record crop produced good but not great wines.

Sonoma County Similar overall weather conditions to those in the Napa Valley, although flowering was later and temperatures cooler and more humid, resulting in considerable powdery mildew. September rains delayed the harvest and many white grapes were lost to bunch-rot. The Cabernet harvest was saved by an Indian summer, producing ripe, fruity wines.

Overall, the exceptionally long harvest produced a huge crop of grapes.

Initially tannic, the Cabernets developed well and are probably at their peak now. Some excellent Zinfandels.

1981 at best ★★★

The earliest harvest on record in almost all areas of California, following a summer of extreme heat.

Napa Valley Budding and flowering were both early and healthy, but Cabernet Sauvignon grapes suffered during the hottest June throughout the USA and large quantities of the crop were lost as a result.

The main harvest was well underway by mid-August. The weather cooled in September, though this was followed by an Indian summer, during which some *Botrytis*-affected grapes were picked and made some fine late-harvest whites.

Overall this was a fairly good year; the white wines were generally better than the reds which tended to be rather light.

Sonoma County Similar weather conditions to the Napa Valley plus hot, dry winds which dried out and concentrated the grapes. This was the shortest growing season on record. The Chardonnays, because of the rapid sugar accumulation, lacked fruit, while the same leanness proved to be rather more attractive in the Cabernets.

Drink up.

1980★★★★

Napa Valley A wet winter was followed by one of the coolest growing seasons on record. Growers feared that sugar levels might be too low but hopes were revived with warm pre-harvest weather. The wines were intense and fruity, bearing comparison with classic European wines.

Sonoma County A similar weather pattern to Napa. The spring suffered some localised hail damage and the pollination period high winds, resulting in a poor flowering and low yields.

Acidity levels were surprisingly high, even after a week of very hot October weather, and balanced well against sugar levels, resulting in some excellent white wines. The Cabernet grapes dehydrated in the high temperatures, and produced concentrated, powerful wines.

Good results despite difficult conditions. Tannic, long-lasting reds, but all the best should be consumed within the next 5–10 years.

1970s NAPA VALLEY

1979★★★ started hot but the cool growing season and September rain necessitated early picking. The best wines were no more than good and did not match the best '78s. **1978★★★★** started with heavy rains which benefited the vines, and developed into a warm growing season. A big crop; the wines were ripe and well-balanced, some were excellent, and the best are drinking well but will develop further.

1977★★ was the second of two years of drought but growers were better prepared for the associated problems. The weather was cooler than 1976 and overall some good wines were made. High sugar and low acidity characterised the wines of **1976★★★** which ranged from poor to good: drink soon.

1975★★★ had a good growing season with some light harvest rains; these were fine, well-balanced, elegant wines.

The star of the decade was undoubtedly **1974★★★★★** arguably the best-ever vintage for California. Growing conditions were ideal: a cool, slightly frosty spring, a long cool summer and perfect harvesting weather. These were excellent, well-balanced wines, but some now starting to tire.

1973★★★★ also enjoyed good growing conditions and a record crop of healthy, perfectly mature grapes produced some very good wines.

The first three vintages of the decade were not of the same calibre as those of the middle years. **1972★** to ★★★★ was a very variable vintage, some very good reds. **1971★★★** was better, the fruit was healthy but the wines were never better than good. Severe spring frosts destroyed half of the **1970★★★★** crop although what was left was generally sound – the best wines were the Cabernets, some of which were very good – overall, though, a very mixed year.

PACIFIC NORTHWEST
(WASHINGTON & OREGON)

ALTHOUGH CONVENIENTLY TWINNED UNDER THE Pacific Northwest heading, the local climate and geography of the vineyard areas of these two neighbouring states could not be more contrasting. The valleys of western Oregon enjoy a mild climate, but weather conditions vary considerably over the growing season, not unlike the maritime climate of Bordeaux, whilst inland, the vineyards of eastern Washington State are in a broad, arid, semi-desert valley, the vines being irrigated by the waters of the Columbia River.

In Oregon, more northerly, more temperate than California, Pinot Noir has – in theory at least – found a natural home, as have the more characteristically acidic Sauvignon Blanc and Riesling. However, Chardonnay, Merlot and Cabernet Sauvignon are also planted in what are relatively new wine areas. The pioneers of the early 1960s have been augmented by a host of mainly small, highly individual wineries, quality equally variable. The wines of both Oregon and Washington State are worth keeping track of.

1991

Washington★★★ An extremely severe winter freeze killed some and damaged many other vines, reducing the potential crop by up to 50%. However, the growing season was satisfactory, the harvest taking place in balmy autumn weather resulting in good sugar and acid levels.

Oregon★★★★ A cold wet spring and very late flowering made up for by a virtually perfect summer and early autumn. A high yield crop of ripe grapes harvested in hot sun before heavy late October rains.

Riesling and Chardonnay ready for drinking now–1995; Merlot, Cabernet and Pinot Noir need 3–6 years bottle-age.

1990

Washington★★★ Cool weather during the flowering cut the crop. Very high temperatures during July and August actually slowed down the ripening of the grapes and the harvest took place early, starting on September 7, running through to October 10. September was unusually warm and those who picked quickly and promptly when the fruit peaked produced excellent, balanced wines. The smallest yield per acre since 1985.

Oregon★★★ The yield per acre was very low here also, although quantities were higher than in 1989 as a result of new plantations. Here too, the spring was cool, but the small crop of unusually small berries yielded some wines of great intensity and depth. Picking began in late September. This was a better year for the Chardonnay than the Pinot Noir, which is usually the most important grape in Oregon.

Rieslings now, Chardonnay soon, the best reds earlier than usual, say, 1994–98.

1989

Washington★★★★ The cool spring and early summer resulted in a moderate sized crop. Grapes developed slowly but steadily until late August. Thereafter growers enjoyed an extraordinary period of hot, sunny days and cool nights, which provided ideal ripening conditions. The harvest began in mid-September and lasted until late October. The wines had exceptional concentration and acidity and the reds show all the potential of a great vintage.

Oregon★★★ A warm, late May and early June brought the vines into early flowering. Mid-June was wet; most vines had set by then but those on higher land set during the rain and consequently the yields were low and variable. Picking began slightly earlier than usual and took place in perfect conditions. Most Pinot Noirs were brought in at optimum maturity; if picked too late they tended to lack finesse and delicacy. Overall, very high quality wines.

White wines all ready for drinking. The top Pinot Noirs from, say, now to 1998.

1988

Washington★★★★ An excellent combination of quantity and quality. A smooth viticultural year with very favourable and normal weather at all times, which produced a large vintage of remarkably even quality. The harvest began on September 8 and ended on October 20. The wines had excellent fruit and good natural balance. The reds should age very well.

Oregon★★★ A cool, wet spring and summer, but with warmer weather during flowering in May. Temperatures rose in mid-July and remained warm through to the middle of September. The yield was down by 50%.

Whites fully mature. Merlot, Cabernet and Pinot Noir now–1996.

1987

Washington★★★★ The hottest summer in 20 years which yielded a very large vintage. The grapes were beautifully ripe and in perfect health when the harvest began on August 28. The better reds were attractive and fruity but have aged more rapidly than is typical for a Washington vintage.

Oregon★★ to ★★★ Here too, with the exception of some cooler weather during July and August, temperatures were high throughout the growing season. Picking took place in hot, dry weather and yields were high throughout Oregon. Quality, however, varied; the best wines were made by the growers who picked early and managed to retain good levels of acidity in their grapes.

Any remaining whites need drinking. Reds now mature.

1986

Washington★★ The warm summer weather ripened the grapes and produced a large vintage. The harvest, which began on September 5, was briefly interrupted by rain; overall the grapes were healthy but the wet weather increased yields in some areas with the result that the wines lack intensity of flavour. The grapes left, unaffected by the rain, produced some very good wines.

Oregon★★ to ★★★★ A wet but sunny start to the year was followed by warm, dry weather through to the harvest. Heavy rain caused some growers to panic, but conditions improved in

October. Yields were average and those who held back the harvest until well after the rains, picked mature grapes and produced the best wines.

Some of the top Pinot Noirs, like Eyrie, still drinking well. Otherwise, drink up.

1985

Washington★★★★ The second of two small crops resulting from unusual spring frosts. The vintage was warm enough for an early harvest, interrupted for a very short while by a cool spell in early September. The reds were big and tannic; the best wines from grapes picked early with high acidity levels.

Oregon★★★★ After a cool, dry start to the year temperatures rose in late May. Early June saw some rain but thereafter the weather was warm and dry, providing excellent conditions for flowering. The growing season and harvest enjoyed the same good conditions and the vintage was mainly completed by mid-October. Quantity was average and the wines showed real ageing potential. This was a vintage which increased international recognition of Oregon wines.

Mainly fully mature.

1984

Washington★★ A very uneven year. Crops were damaged by winter frost and the cool spring weather further diminished the yield. Summer saw good, sunny weather and autumn was dry but cooler than usual. Despite this the crop ripened satisfactorily and some good wines were made, although quality varied.

Oregon★ As with the Washington vintage, this was a variable year. The first five months were exceptionally wet; temperatures rose in May but this encouraged mildew. Fruit set did not complete until well into July. Thereafter temperatures were low and the harvest was held back until November in the hope that conditions would improve: they did not. A large crop of light wines.

Few seen. Drink up.

1983

Washington★★★★ A cool year, but late summer and autumn provided some warm, sunny ripening weather. Picking began on September 19. A brief frost caused damage to some vineyards in lower lying areas, but the better-located sites made exceptionally concentrated, lively wines. A very good year for red wines with charming fruit and excellent structure giving fine potential for ageing.

Oregon★★★★ The vines flowered in June in perfect weather and thereafter the season was warm and dry with some benign rainfall in late August. Picking took place during the first fortnight of October. A larger than average crop; some growers waited too long before picking but otherwise these were wines with good ageing potential.

Whites now too old. Reds fully mature; drink up.

1982

Washington★★ The vines flowered in good conditions and a warm summer was followed by a cool and extended harvest, beginning September 21 and ending November 9, with some rain. Charming but lightish wines. Many of the better reds have lasted well and shown good character, but lack intensity.

Oregon★★★ After a cool, wet spring the weather was perfect for flowering in June. Thereafter trouble-free conditions prevailed for the remainder of the year and picking was complete by early October. These were very good wines which, nevertheless, will last less well than the 1983 vintage, despite having the acidity needed for ageing.

Drink up.

1981

Washington★★★ The cool, damp weather at the start of the year held through to flowering, limiting the size of the crop, but warm summer weather helped advance development. Cool autumn nights and warm days fully ripened the grapes and picking began September 21. These were fruity, substantial wines; the reds showed great depth and potential longevity.

Oregon★★★ The months leading to July were generally cool, then wet weather retarded flowering until mid-July. As in Washington, warm, sunny weather advanced development until late September when the rain returned. Picking began in early October and the yield was very low. These were wines which would reveal their worth with long keeping.

The better Pinot Noirs holding up. Best to drink soon.

1980

Washington★★★ The eruption of Mount St Helens blanketed in ash many vineyards throughout this region of the US, but fortunately this occurred prior to flowering.

This was the coolest growing season of the 1980s, and, indeed, vineyards had not entirely recovered from the severe freeze of 1978/79 – consequently the crop was small and the wines were light; many, though, were well-balanced with moderate body. The best reds had good ageing potential.

Oregon★★★★ Cold, wet weather prevailed throughout the spring until June. Here too, vineyards were covered with large deposits of ash from the volcano, but vines were left undamaged. A late flowering finished in July. Picking began in early October producing a very small crop of excellent, concentrated, dry wines.

Attractive, rich, root-like, earthy, true Pinot varietal character, doubtless peaked by now.

EARLIER VINTAGES

Earlier vintages hard to come by but the **1979** Amity and Knudson-Erath Pinot Noirs were showing well in the mid-1980s. The few wines that were made in the 1960s, if any exist, will be no more than curiosities. Times – and winemaking – have moved on.

NEW YORK STATE

IT WILL COME AS A SURPRISE TO MOST EUROPEANS
that New York is a wine producing state, so dominant is
California. Wines have in fact been made in the Finger Lakes
district, just south of Ontario, for well over a century, though
until the early 1960s only native American varieties, not the
species *Vitis vinifera*, and hybrids were grown.

Virtually the sole pioneer of classic European grape
varieties was the late Dr Konstantin Frank, followed in the
1970s by one or two small wineries such as Glenora and Heron
Hill, planting first Riesling, then Chardonnay. In the mid-1970s
there was a revival of winemaking in the less northerly, less
exposed Hudson Valley, and, even more recently, with classic
whites and reds planted on sea-girt Long Island.

New pioneers, enthusiasts and state-of-the-art winemaking,
particularly on Long Island, have successfully changed the New
York State wine scene: Pinot Noir, Cabernet Sauvignon,
Sauvignon Blanc and Chardonnay are now produced, though, as
with New Zealand, the reds, though well made, have as yet no
track record.

Wines made from the native American grape varieties such
as Catawba and Concord – very much an acquired taste – and
hybrids like Seibel, are not covered in the brief vintage notes
that follow. The lighter dry whites, as always, should be drunk
while they are young and fresh, though some of the Finger
Lake Chardonnays and late-harvest wines will keep for five
years or more.

1991★★★★

Clearly a well-above average vintage. Unlike California and the
Northwest Pacific a mild winter, early spring and flowering,
warm summer and early harvest. In the northerly Finger Lakes
district the earliest-ever start of harvest, August 27. A large
crop: Riesling and Gewurztraminer were particularly successful.
On Long Island the warm dry vintage was expected to produce
wines to equal the '88s – the best year of the decade – a situation
echoed in the Hudson River Valley.
Drink whites soon. Reds now–1996.

1990★★★★

A very good vintage. With the exception of the Finger Lakes
where yields were good, crop size was slightly below average
due to the dry growing season in 1988, the large crop in 1989,
and cool weather during the fruit set of this year. Rainfall was
above average but well-distributed and this contributed to good
berry size. Ideal ripening weather in September led to a harvest
several weeks earlier than normal for some grape varieties, still
measuring the same sugar levels as the previous year.

Overall, the grapes were clean and healthy, promising wines
of very good quality.
Whites drinking now. Reds now–1995.

1989★★ to ★★★

Following the 1988 drought, groundwater levels were low until
late spring rains began; these threatened disease but stopped
before it was too late. This and heavy sporadic rainfall,

particularly bad in Hudson River and eastern Long Island, coupled with the effects of Hurricane Hugo on Long Island, made 1989 a difficult year for many. However, improved techniques and careful timing helped to overcome problems.

Overall, the early-ripening varieties fared best, making this a good year for sparkling and white table wines. Those from the Lake Erie region had very good varietal character, and Hudson Valley growers considered the quality of their grapes to be excellent having fought against such difficult weather conditions; not one of the best years for Long Island wines though.

Drink soon.

1988★★★★★

Deemed 'a winemaker's dream' by James Tresize, President of the New York Wine & Grape Foundation. Growers enjoyed dry weather and a perfect summer and autumn: warm days and cool nights. With the exception of grapes left for late harvest, and ice-wines, the vintage and 'crush' was complete by mid-October. Total yield was down by 12% due to the dry weather and grapes were perfectly clean and healthy.

A vintage of powerful, distinctive wines; it was the best year since 1980 for the reds and the whites alike.

Drink whites now. Best reds now–1996.

1987★★ to ★★★★

A year which ranged from average to very good, but was overshadowed by the two superior vintages on either side. Growers experienced occasional adverse weather conditions, including strong winds in mid-September on Long Island which dampened hopes for a trouble-free harvest, and wet weather throughout that month in many areas. Grapes had, however, ripened well until then and the harvest was already two weeks ahead of schedule, so adverse effects were minimised.

This was a well-structured vintage; Long Island wineries reported better success with reds than whites, while in the Finger Lakes winemakers reported the reverse. Overall, however, the Seyval Blanc and red *vinifera* varieties were considered to be the most consistent.

Whites should have been consumed by now. Reds now–1995.

1986★ to ★★★

A poor year for many growers whose crops were spoilt by a wet harvest. There were, however, some exceptions. Long Island growers considered this to be a very good vintage, their wines were typically aromatic, the whites had good colour, were smooth and had lingering finishes; their reds showed good ageing potential. A good year also for Lake Erie, a Chardonnay from this district ranked second among 223 Chardonnays from around the world in the 1987 Intervin International Competition.

Whites too old. Reds, drink soon.

1985★★★

Generally very good, except for Long Island where vines were devastated by Hurricane Gloria which struck on September 27. Until then it had been a fine vintage; the Chardonnay had just ripened and made it to the cellars, the Sauvignon Blanc was nipped in the bud, as was the Cabernet Sauvignon. Those with skill, however, made good wines.

Drink soon.

1984★★★

The second of two unusually large crops. Quality varied depending on the grape variety and the region. In the Finger Lakes most early varieties had a problem-free harvest but a severe frost on October 6 virtually stopped the later grapes from ripening further. However, in the Hudson River the later varieties did well. Overall, the Seyval Blanc and Chardonnay made the best quality wines.

1984 is also the year that marked a transition in New York State away from the dessert wines and red wines towards the dry whites and sparkling wines, and away from the native American grape varieties towards those of *Vitis vinifera*.

Drink up.

EARLIER VINTAGES

Long Island enjoyed an Indian summer in **1983★★★★** and produced deeply coloured wines which were exceptionally soft when young, though not for ageing.

1982★★★★★ and **1980★★★★** saw good wines, and **1981★** a small crop of indifferent quality.

Some pre-1980 vintages of above average quality include: **1979** (Rieslings), **1978** (Riesling, Chardonnay and late-harvest Gewurztraminer), **1976** (Cabernet Sauvignon), and **1975** (Chardonnay and late-harvest Riesling). All will be past best.

AUSTRALIA

AUSTRALIA IS A CONTINENT, ALBEIT A SPARSELY populated one. The wine areas are far apart, the oldest classic district, the Hunter Valley in New South Wales, being some 1,287 kilometres (800 miles) from the newest vineyard sites of Western Australia; the cooler regions: Coonawarra and Tasmania are in the south. Confusingly, it is normal practice to make good red wine blended from different grape varieties grown in different regions.

Though vine growing and winemaking dates back to the penal colony days of the early 19th century, the demand was for fortified and, frankly, undistinguished table wines. Thanks to new attitudes and new techniques, to brilliant pioneers, imaginative wine education and publicity, the past 20 years or so have witnessed a quality revolution. The results are instantly appealing Chardonnays, impressive reds, straight Cabernets and Shiraz' and well-constructed blends, fruity Rieslings, and idiosyncratic Semillons – not to mention luscious Muscats and very good sparkling wines.

However, unlike the more temperate and stable regions of northern Europe the weather in Australia can fluctuate between extremes of heat and drought and excessive torrential rain. Vintage variations can be correspondingly dramatic.

1992★ to ★★★

This was one of the most difficult vintages of the past twenty years, making generalisations hazardous: some very good, possibly great, wines will eventuate, but also will some very ordinary ones.

New South Wales A region subject to very different weather patterns to those of southern Australia, the Hunter Valley's harvest is one to two months earlier.

This year was one to forget: a severe winter and spring drought sharply reduced potential yields, and was followed by heavy rain throughout harvesting. The odd Semillon, a few of the Chardonnays, and the occasional Cabernet will succeed, but should be chosen carefully.

South Australia The coolest summer since records began well over a century ago; powdery mildew appeared on a scale not seen since 1974. Three periods of rain – early March, end of March, and late April – turned vintage time into a game of Russian Roulette. Those who guessed correctly have made some wonderfully intense and aromatic wines; those who got caught by mildew and/or rain have fared poorly.

Victoria Similar summer weather, the coolest this century, but missing the rain. From northeast Victoria (superb Muscat and 'Tokay') through to the Yarra Valley in the south (great Pinot Noir), the state's 200 vignerons have smiles broadened further by the good though not excessive yields.

Western Australia Again with the same viticultural vexations of South Australia. Yields were high, as were expectations, but rain during vintage caused headaches for many vignerons: it has to be remembered that like California, most Australian regions expect (and are blessed by) dry growing and harvest seasons. The white wines suffered most; some good Cabernets produced in the south, though, will almost certainly redeem the situation.

Too early to say.

1991★★★★

A generally warm and dry vintage produced smaller than usual crops, and wines of power and concentration; for some regions a better year than 1990, but not for all.

New South Wales For once the Hunter Valley had a good growing season, and this was followed by a dry vintage. Fleshy, rich wines which will give tremendous pleasure early in their lives; but which may not be particularly long-lasting – especially the whites.

South Australia A wet spring followed by a dry, warm summer and autumn. Yields were down on 1990 by 10–30%, with the red wines most affected. The compensation was great depth of colour and extract, although time will show whether they have the vinous heart of the best of the '90s.

Victoria Much the same conditions as South Australia, with yields down by 15–33%. All regions – of which there are a dozen – had a relatively early start in March, and moved through to the end of April in benign conditions, making lush, concentrated wines which will provide a great contrast to the more elegant but lighter wines of 1990.

Western Australia Vintage time for the whole of Australia is led by the Swan Valley with its January commencement. This year the Swan had a mild (relatively speaking) year, producing high quality wines.

Regions further south experienced a Swan Valley-like heatwave in early February, which was most damaging in the lower Great Southern region, but which did not prevent some of the top vineyards making lovely wines from yields down by 15–40% on average levels, and which had much less impact in the Margaret River.

The whites are rich, full-flavoured wines which should develop quite soon, the best will have cellaring capability. The reds are rich and concentrated and will need considerable bottle-ageing.

1990★★★★

A good growing season for most of the regions in Australia and a mild summer suggested that this would be a vintage with relatively high natural acid levels, and hence would be suitable for cellaring.

New South Wales A wet winter followed by excellent conditions during the spring and summer. Bud-break, flowering and fruit set all took place in ideal conditions. However, around harvest time rainfall was heavy, diluting the Chardonnay and Semillon in the Lower Hunter Valley and consequently increasing the yield. The later-harvested reds were less affected, but overall, this was an uneven year.

South Australia A wet spring in most areas, particularly Coonawarra, was followed by a cool summer. Vines then suffered some stress during dry weather throughout the growing season. Picking began early in the Barossa Valley thanks to the supply and quality of the Pinot Noir. Generally, average yields. Winegrowers in the Adelaide Hills judged this to be their best vintage for three years.

Victoria A generally good growing season, with cool temperatures and two good falls of rain in the western areas. Humidity caused the odd problem, particularly in the Yarra Valley, but disease was kept under control. Growers held out until the end of March for their Cabernets, anticipating a very special vintage. Yields were up by 20%.

Western Australia Mild weather during the summer provided good growing conditions. Picking began around mid-March, later in the Swan Valley. Late February rains caused some bunch rot in the later ripening grapes, particularly the Chenin Blanc. Yields were above average in Margaret River, but lower than usual in the Swan Valley. Overall, however, the quality was good.

Dry whites mainly ready for drinking. The reds, newly bottled, need appropriate cellaring time.

1989★ to ★★★

After five highly successful years, this vintage came as something of a disappointment to Australian winemakers.

New South Wales The Upper Hunter Valley harvested first after a wet spring, dry summer and further wet weather just before picking. In the Lower Hunter Valley rain delayed the harvest. The whites are no more than satisfactory. A mediocre year for the Cabernets, better for Shiraz.

South Australia High rainfall in the Barossa Valley was followed by three months of dry weather from January onwards. A cool growing season produced healthy vines, and a heatwave in early March reduced the yield but, where irrigation was used, did not affect the wines. Overall, a good but not great year. The best wines were the Rhine Rieslings and the Chardonnays.

In Coonawarra growing conditions were also very good, except for some rainfall later on in the vintage causing minor *Botrytis* in the later ripening grapes. Overall, the white wines had good character, those late-harvested being light but fruity and elegant.

Victoria A very problematic year. A very windy spring in the Yarra Valley meant a bad fruit set which seriously diminished crops. Apart from the odd period of hot weather the summer was mild and wet, leading to widespread rot. Nevertheless, some fine wines were made, in particular deep-coloured, flavoury Pinot Noirs and attractive Chardonnays. Other wines tended to be rather unripe and light.

In Milawa better conditions, combined with modern technology, made this a more successful vintage, with some excellent Muscats. There were, however, some casualties: bad harvest weather forced early picking and consequently no 'noble' late-harvest Rieslings were made. Cabernets were picked earlier than usual and they tended to produce finer, lighter wines.

Western Australia An easier year generally. A hot, early vintage in the Swan Valley turned cool, resulting in light wines. In Margaret River cool weather and heavy rainfall in mid-January and February caused some *Botrytis* in the Rhine Rieslings but this was arrested by dry, warm weather conditions in March.

The white grapes generally made good wines with high acid levels, particularly in the Chardonnays and Semillons; and the red grapes produced wines which have good fruit flavours and show much promise.

The fragrant Rieslings and Gewurztraminers are delicious now. The bigger Chardonnays, though, need a year or so more bottle-age. The best of the Shiraz' should be splendid around 1994–98.

1988★★ to ★★★★

Overall, a year which produced some exceptional wines, despite difficult weather conditions.

New South Wales In the Upper Hunter Valley, a warm, wet winter followed by a mild growing season, enabled growers to pick early before the rains came. In the Lower Hunter, however, the harvest was delayed and rain nearly ruined the vintage. The yield was above average though and this region produced subtle, elegant wines.

South Australia Weather conditions in the Barossa Valley for this year followed a similar pattern to those in New South Wales, but included a hailstorm on October 14 which cost some growers up to 50% of their crop. On the whole, though, a large yield of good wines.

Further south, in Coonawarra, the dry, warm weather necessitated irrigation and resulted in the earliest vintage of the decade. Yields had been slashed by September frosts but quality was correspondingly enhanced.

Victoria An excellent year for Milawa. Perfect weather conditions produced outstanding Shiraz, and the late harvest proved ideal for dessert wines, including some very promising liqueur Muscats.

Western Australia Hail and high winds in the spring plus excessive heat in the summer made this a difficult year in Margaret River. The Rieslings and Cabernet Sauvignons tended to lack acidity but, conversely, earlier varieties showed good ripeness and balance.

The light, dry, fruity white wines should be drunk now. Heavier Chardonnays, however, can take a year or two more bottle-age. The top reds should be ready for drinking, say, now–2000.

1987★★★★

An excellent vintage throughout Australia, for both red and white wines alike.

New South Wales Apart from heavy rain in October/ November in the Upper Hunter Valley, followed by very cold weather which disrupted flowering, conditions were on the whole very good.

South Australia Heavy hailstorms in the Barossa region diminished the potential yield of the earlier varieties, including the Chardonnays and the Pinot Noirs. Then high winds here and in Coonawarra pruned the crop further. Thereafter conditions were generally good during the summer months and the harvest began late – in mid-May in Coonawarra where quality was not quite up to that of the previous year. Otherwise, this was an elegant vintage.

Victoria Apart from a poor fruit set in the Yarra Valley, which resulted in yields reduced by 30–50%, vintage conditions were very good.

Western Australia Here too good conditions prevailed. A mild spring saw good bud-break, and cool weather during the growing season resulted in a late vintage. High yields, high quality.

Wonderfully luscious Chardonnays, delicious for drinking now. The lighter Semillons, Sauvignon Blancs and Rieslings: drink up. Shiraz and Pinot Noir developing well; the Cabernets can be kept.

1986★★★★★

A consistently good vintage throughout Australia, possibly the best of the decade.

New South Wales An extremely wet winter in the Hunter Valley followed by a damp, mild spring resulting in an excellent fruit set and flowering. Dry weather held until early June but mild temperatures allowed the grapes to ripen slowly. Picking began ten days late and conditions were excellent for the sweet wines. Long-lived, tannic reds and superb Semillons.

South Australia A mild winter and spring in Barossa. Temperatures during the growing season in the hills were the lowest on record, but rose everywhere in time for the harvest. Rain in mid-April encouraged the development of *Botrytis* on the late ripening Rieslings. Here too there were some superbly balanced, powerful, stylish wines.

Victoria Again, a cool growing season. The summer saw the lowest seasonal temperatures on record; grapes in Milawa ripened very late so that some of the normally late varieties were ready for picking before the earlier varieties.

Western Australia Overall, conditions were very similar to those in the rest of Australia. There were exceptions, including a tropical cyclone in the Swan Valley, making February here the wettest on record. Yields here were down by 20%. Heavy showers diluted sugar levels during the harvest in some very localised areas of Margaret River.

Chardonnays of the quality and style that have put Australia right into the top league; lovely now. Perfect late-harvest Rieslings and substantial reds, Grange Hermitage superb and needing considerably more bottle-age. All the best reds will last until, possibly beyond, 2000.

1985★★★★

As with 1986, this was another consistently good year throughout Australia, although largely overshadowed by the vintages on either side.

New South Wales Good growing conditions in the Hunter Valley, with high temperatures in January, brought the harvest forward to the middle of the month. In the Lower Hunter Valley a January hailstorm caused a loss of up to 30% of the crop.

South Australia Heavy rains in Barossa during spring saw good development of the vines but a summer drought caused problems for unirrigated estates. Late March rains caused further problems with powdery mildew. Sugar levels were below normal in Coonawarra due to cool weather, but the conditions allowed the later varieties to ripen perfectly. South Australia saw its largest ever crop, due largely to the introduction of new vineyards.

Victoria The coolest ripening season in Milawa for years was followed by a warm Indian summer. The harvest finished in May, producing grapes with high sugar levels. Heavy rain during harvest in the Yarra Valley though, reduced yields by as much as 50%, but grapes brought in prior to this made good wines.

Western Australia The wines from the Margaret River were the stars of the 1985 vintage. High winds damaged vines during flowering, and fruit set and cool temperatures prevailed until late February. Picking, however, took place in ideal conditions.

*A strange coincidence that '85s in the southern hemisphere
are as agreeably fruity and balanced as the '85s made in
France. Attractive, rich but easy young reds, rich now.
Chardonnays fully mature. Late-picked dessert wines and
Muscats, delicious.*

1984★★★★

The first of a run of elegant, stylish Australian vintages.
   New South Wales Unlike most of Australia, the Hunter
Valley did not enjoy a good year. Vines were damaged in the
Upper Hunter by Christmas and New Year storms, then hail.
Conditions were better in the Lower Hunter Valley where cool
weather encouraged excellent development. Rain later on,
however, caused mildew and rot.
   South Australia Despite a wet start to the year the yield
was low in Barossa, still suffering from the effects of the
previous year's drought. The cool summer and autumn
encouraged good levels of *Botrytis* on the grapes, making this
an excellent year for the production of late-harvest wines.
Outstanding Cabernet and Shiraz.
   Victoria Stable conditions in Milawa and a trouble-free
vintage. In the Yarra Valley cool, wet weather throughout the
year delayed the harvest; some fine late-harvest wines were
produced.
   Western Australia Apart from a lack of late rain in the
Margaret River region, and a cooler than normal growing
season in the Swan Valley, this was a trouble-free year.
   *Most of the dry whites should have been consumed by now
but those of the quality of Lindemans' Padthaway and Tyrell's
Vat 47 will still be delicious. The reds are good but not great.
The late-harvest Rieslings are still superb.*

1983★★

An excellent vintage for some, but most areas were dogged by
disastrous weather conditions.
   New South Wales The third year of drought in the Hunter
Valley, reducing yields to below 50% of normal in the Upper
Hunter. In the Lower Hunter the vintage was salvaged by
torrential rain at bud-burst. Some excellent reds and rich, full-
flavoured Semillons and Chardonnays.
   South Australia The long drought in the Barossa region
ended halfway through the vintage with widespread flooding, a
carpet of mud and debris covering many vineyards. In
Coonawarra conditions were better, with the exception of late
rains around the harvest. Variable quality.
   Victoria An early vintage in Milawa followed a cool
growing season and a hot spell in February. A year of disasters
in the Yarra Valley: October frosts, November hailstorms, a
summer-long drought and an invasion of European wasps all
caused considerable damage.
   Western Australia In contrast to the rest of Australia, 1983
was a near-perfect year in the Margaret River region; weather
conditions throughout the growing season were excellent, and
the vintage ended with two benign falls of rain in February.
Yields were up by 10%.
   *Despite dramatic weather conditions some lovely golden
Chardonnays and some velvety Pinot Noirs and Cabernets.
Most are ready for drinking, many past their best.*

1982★★★★

Near-perfect conditions in most areas produced some well-balanced, stylish wines.

New South Wales Good levels of rainfall throughout the spring and summer in the Hunter Valley brought an end to the drought. This was followed by warm to hot weather which enabled fruit to ripen well.

South Australia Good spring rains in the Barossa Valley counter-balanced high temperatures in January and February. A late harvest, continuing until May, produced some excellent wines. Coonawarra enjoyed a stable year and produced Cabernets with exceptional ageing potential.

Victoria A mild growing season was followed by rains delaying the harvest in Milawa. An average sized yield.

In the Yarra Valley the cool, dry summer enabled fruit to ripen well and an above average yield was brought in. Again, a very good year.

Western Australia Margaret River saw its coolest growing season for many years with much frost damage. In the Swan Valley it was a cool, stable year producing wines of good fruit.

Buttery Chardonnays and superb late-harvest Rieslings, all ripe and ready when young; should have been consumed by now. Superlative reds: Penfolds' Bin 707 Cabernet Sauvignon, and the mainly Shiraz, Grange Hermitage with years of life ahead of them.

1981★★

A difficult and generally unpopular year. The hot, early vintage produced dull wines, both red and white, which never really improved with age.

New South Wales A serious drought throughout the Hunter Valley drastically reduced yields.

South Australia Winemakers of the Barossa Valley harvested their grapes early. The yield was very small and, as a result of the drought, the berries were small and of uneven quality. Coonawarra, however, missed the worst of this and experienced a slightly better year.

Victoria Mild, occasionally hot weather in Milawa led to an early harvest, taking place in ideal conditions. Some good red wines were made.

Western Australia Poor weather disrupted flowering in Margaret River and yields were further reduced by high winds in late spring. Thereafter conditions were good. The Swan Valley had few problems and the crop was brought in in excellent condition.

Drink up.

1980★★★★

A vintage with an excellent reputation, especially for Cabernets.

New South Wales In all parts of the Hunter Valley an exceptionally hot and dry year. Picking began several weeks earlier than usual, beginning January 11 in the Lower Hunter and continuing into early March. No problems with rot or mildew, but drought resulted in a very low yield.

South Australia In both Barossa and Coonawarra this was a trouble-free year which produced a large crop of grapes. The Cabernets have excellent ageing potential.

Victoria Described as a 'copybook year' in Milawa for all styles from table to dessert wine. In the Yarra Valley a severe year-long drought produced a small crop of good, ripe fruit to make excellent wines of all styles.

Western Australia A dry year in Margaret River where winemaking was still in its infancy. In the Swan Valley a mild to warm year produced evenly-ripened fruit.

The whites should have been consumed by now but the beefy, tannic Cabernets are still developing.

1970s

Prior to 1980 it is safe to say that the white wines will be well past their best, but Cabernet Sauvignon, the best Shiraz, and blended reds can still be superb.

Star ratings for top reds: **1979★★★★ 1978★★★★ 1977★★★ 1976★★★★ 1975★★★★★ 1974★ 1973★★★★ 1972~ 1971★★★★★**

1960s

The decade of the 1960s was one of development, the market dominated by the bigger, well-established producers such as Lindemans and Penfolds.

Best years for Cabernet and Shiraz: **1967★★★ 1966★★★★★ 1965★★ 1963★★★★ 1962★★★★★ 1960★★** – all fully mature.

NEW ZEALAND

OF ALL THE SO-CALLED 'NEW WORLD' WINES, NEW Zealand's are the newest and, in relation to appeal, quality and price, most successful. Prior to 1970 New Zealand was noted for sheep, butter and beautiful, uncrowded countryside. Then vines were planted and, throughout the 1980s, dramatic advances were made.

Several things must be borne in mind. New Zealand is not a 'district' but two large islands, each with its own vineyard areas. The wine zones stretch roughly 1,207 kilometres (750 miles) north to south and the variations in vintage quality are often considerable. In 1988, for example, the Gisborne wine region was devastated by a subtropical storm while, under 322 kilometres (200 miles) away, Marlborough and Martinborough enjoyed well-nigh perfect conditions. New Zealand's weather is strongly influenced by the surrounding oceans. These moderate the temperature range – both diurnal and seasonal. However, the country is exposed to both subtropical and subpolar climatic influences, which make the weather conditions from year to year extremely variable.

1992★★★★

Potentially good, though crop below average in some districts.

A cool, windy spring delayed flowering and caused *millerandage* reducing the anticipated harvest. The fallout from the Mount Pinatubo eruptions continued to bring atmospheric disturbance throughout the 1991/2 growing season, helping to reduce sunshine levels and temperatures throughout the summer.

Prior to and during the harvest some fine but cool weather, particularly in the South Island, resulted in grapes of higher than usual acidity, though after a delayed picking, higher than ever sugar levels were recorded in Sauvignon Blanc and Chardonnay grapes in Auckland. Red varietals have good colour and balance.

In Gisborne good quality but low yield Chardonnay and Gewurztraminer. The Hawkes Bay crop was also down and its acidity high, though the wines are expected to turn out well. In Marlborough harvest was good but delayed, the ripest grapes being from stonier soils.

Too early to say.

1991★★★★

A well-above average, though late vintage following variable but generally good weather conditions. By district:

Auckland had a mild, dry spring, though humid towards its end; a windy but dry late summer and autumn gave excellent conditions for fruit ripening, especially for late-harvest varieties.

The neighbouring districts of Gisborne and Hawkes Bay had similar climatic conditions: a windy, cool spring, good fruit set but with quite a lot of rain followed by a late summer. More rain during the harvest dictated slightly early picking of some varieties. Later varieties matured well.

Rain also caused problems in Marlborough and meant some early picking, but overall, a late harvest of excellent ripeness. Advantage was taken of *Botrytis* to make late-harvest Rieslings for which New Zealand is beginning to achieve a reputation.

Whites: for fairly early drinking. Reds: drink around the mid-1990s, the best beyond.

1990★★ to ★★★★

An above average yield of good wines which was rather overshadowed by the previous vintage. Sunny conditions alternated with showers, keeping winemakers on their toes throughout the country, though ultimately most appeared fairly satisfied with their wines.

Auckland harvested their best quality grapes for many years. Summer rain followed by dry, settled conditions during the harvest resulted in good, aromatic wines. Gisborne made good Chardonnays and other later-ripening varieties. Cabernet Sauvignon and Merlot grapes were harvested late in Hawkes Bay and produced wines of good character and maturity, leaving winemakers with high hopes for their red wines of this vintage.

In the South Island, Marlborough's vineyards suffered damage from late frosts. But the Sauvignon Blancs and Chardonnays had high sugar levels and good fruit. Most reds were harvested early. Conversely Canterbury, particularly Waipara Valley, harvested grapes in hot, dry conditions.

Overall, this was a very large, moderately good vintage. Balancing levels of acidity in the Chardonnays make these wines with ageing potential.

Bearing in mind that the harvest in New Zealand takes place in what is spring in the northern hemisphere, the whites are more than ready for drinking. The reds are just starting their serious bottle-ageing and will need time.

1989★★★★★

Declared the 'vintage of the century' by several enthusiastic winemakers. This was certainly an excellent harvest throughout the country.

Abundant sun and heat, near perfect ripening conditions, and a bountiful harvest, produced many top wines from both white and red grapes. Some were, unusually, almost overripe, with high levels of alcohol in the Chardonnays and intense colours and flavours in the reds. The best of both promise to age very well indeed.

Martinborough produced a handful of record-breaking Pinot Noirs, Hawkes Bay an outstanding collection of Cabernet Sauvignons, and Marlborough boasted a 'best ever' vintage.

Sauvignon Blanc drinking now, the best Chardonnay can take further bottle-ageing. Cabernet Sauvignon, say, now–1998.

1988★ to ★★★★

A notoriously variable vintage thanks to a tropical cyclone which devastated Gisborne and severely impaired quality in Auckland and Hawkes Bay. Many Gisborne vineyards were totally submerged by torrential rain and the region was officially declared a disaster area. Nevertheless, some surprisingly palatable wines emerged from even the hardest hit regions, although their quality was eclipsed by the 1989 vintage.

In dramatic contrast, Martinborough experienced one of the hottest and driest years for some time and produced some excellent wines. Marlborough had a good vintage despite some rain at the beginning of the harvest.

Sauvignon Blanc and Gewurztraminer, drink up. Chardonnay, drink soon. The best reds will keep and develop further.

1987★ to ★★★★

Following two abundant harvests, 1987 saw a drop in quantity and quality. Poor fruit set reduced the size of the crop and heavy rain early in the harvest caused further problems. Auckland and Hawkes Bay suffered least but quality was markedly low in the rest of New Zealand. Later varieties were more fortunate as weather conditions improved towards the end of the year.

Most best drunk soon though some Botrytis-*affected sweet wines drinking superbly and will keep.*

1986★★★ to ★★★★★

Wet weather in most areas during January and February got the vintage off to a bad start; early varieties including Müller-Thurgau suffered from rot. Thereafter, the weather cleared and 1986 enjoyed mostly outstanding results from the later-ripening varieties, particularly Chardonnay. Several of the classic New Zealand wines, including Morton Estate Black Label Chardonnay, achieved new heights in wine quality and proved to have real ageing potential.

The red wines responded well to the late summer, although they were not quite as good as the previous year's.

The top Chardonnays superb now and holding well.
Cabernet Sauvignon coming into its own, the best, such as Matua Valley, just about ready though will keep.

1985★★ to ★★★★

A very large vintage which added to a growing wine surplus; as a result the government sponsored a vine extraction scheme the following year.

Heavy rain during the beginning of the harvest caused outbreaks of rot which encouraged many growers to pick their white grapes before optimum ripeness. Even the usually dry Marlborough suffered because of the wet weather and made few memorable wines. The Chardonnay and red grape varieties benefited from better ripening weather late-season to give good results in all areas. The best came from Auckland, the most northerly wine region, and the Southern Canterbury region.

Drink up all except some of the better long-lasting reds.

1984★

An anticlimax after the much-praised 1983 vintage.

Poor fruit set and hail damage in some regions reduced the crop by one-third that of the previous year, despite an increase in the number of vineyards producing wine.

Due to widespread rain and humidity, quality was only average in the North Island regions. The vintage was slightly better in South Island, particularly in Marlborough.

This was certainly not a great year for reds; all varieties suffered from a lack of ripeness and flavour. North Island wines have not aged well. Overall, a below average vintage.

Drink up.

1983★★★★★

A top vintage which combined quality and quantity. Growers everywhere reported excellent results; many claimed this to be their best ever vintage, although advances in viticulture and winemaking were no doubt partly responsible.

Particularly successful were the North Island regions where abundant sunshine and near drought conditions produced grapes with the highest sugar levels in recent memory. The best red wines were from Hawkes Bay and Gisborne, with plenty of colour and flavour intensity and real ageing potential. In the South Island, Marlborough, Nelson and, to a lesser extent, Canterbury, had a successful vintage, although quantities were lower than from the North Island.

Whites should have been drunk. Most good reds at peak but will keep.

1982★ to ★★★

An average vintage; the wines varied considerably from region to region.

Hot, dry conditions towards the end of the growing season favoured red grape varieties, particularly in Hawkes Bay and Canterbury. 1982 saw the creation of two classic red wines, Te Mata Coleraine and St Helena Pinot Noir, both of which had good ageing potential.

Gisborne and Auckland suffered from rain and a lack of sunshine early in the season, and as the poor conditions continued, with heavy rain in February and March, some producers lost heart and picked their grapes too early and, predictably, produced poor wines, the reds lacking in colour, flavour and longevity.

Whites now all long consumed. Even the best reds need drinking.

1981★★

A poor flowering and fruit set was followed by a fairly dry, but rather sunless, growing season. The harvest yielded a small crop of clean but rather unripe grapes.

Marlborough, Canterbury and Hawkes Bay were the stars of the vintage. Later varieties, especially the reds, benefited most from sunnier conditions towards the end of the harvest.

Several Cabernet Sauvignons from this vintage have survived a decade of maturation but show green and leafy characteristics. This is typical of wines from a period before better site selection and improved viticulture produced far superior grapes.

Drink up.

1980★

Wet weather affected most regions during the growing season, including the normally dry region of Marlborough. Canterbury and, to a lesser extent, Hawkes Bay escaped the worst of the rain at harvest time. Many grapes were picked prematurely, however, to avoid rot. This resulted in wines which lacked ripeness and longevity.

Overall, this was a poor year for reds, but the whites fared a little better. High acidity and bunch rot characterised the worst.

Few remain. Drink up.

THE CAPE

CAPE WINES CAN HARDLY BE CALLED 'NEW WORLD' wines. Vines were planted and wine made by the earliest Dutch settlers of this region in the late 17th century. During the next century the wines of Constantia were renowned – fashionable and highly priced – but, like madeira, fell out of favour as the 19th century progressed. Indifferent table and fortified wines were made, the principal export until well into the 1950s being good, inexpensive sherry-type wines. The renaissance of fine table wines began in the 1960s and 1970s though was largely unnoticed or, for political reasons, ignored. Over the past decade or so, great strides have been made in the selection of cultivars (vine varieties), winemaking and effective wine control systems.

Over a dozen red cultivars are grown in the Cape, of which Pinotage, Cabernet Sauvignon and Pinot Noir are the best known, and around 15 white cultivars, the most widely planted being the versatile Steen (Chenin Blanc), also Sauvignon Blanc, the increasingly successful Chardonnay, some Gewurztraminer and a small amount of high quality Riesling.

It might be imagined that the Cape enjoys one long hot season after another. Not so. Being the southern tip of South Africa winters can be cold and wet, the Coastal Regions having variable springs and summers. At vertical tastings in the Cape I have noted that potentially hefty reds made with cultivars such as Pinotage are better after a long cool growing season. Notwithstanding, the keeping quality of many reds, even the most commercial brands, is remarkably good. Moreover, the quality/price ratio is very favourable for the consumer.

1992★★★★★

An all-time record crop: over 10 million hectolitres (to put this into perspective, greater than the average for all the vineyards of Germany). Cool conditions during the harvest produced juice with good acidity, excellent taste concentration, good colour in the reds, and intensely flavoured whites: Cabernet Sauvignon of superb quality, a wide range of the increasingly popular and successful Chardonnays, Sauvignon Blancs packed with fruit, and the best-ever Merlots. The only grape varieties to suffer setbacks were the Riesling (Cruchen Blanc) and Rhine Riesling, harvested during a week of mild heatwave in February.

Sauvignon and Chenin Blanc drink soon. Cask-matured reds released from 1983/4 for drinking from, say, 1995 to beyond 2000, depending on quality.

1991★★★★★

The wettest winter on record. May and June also wet, but an early spring was followed by a cool dry summer. Healthy grapes. Great potential.

The lighter drier whites, drink fairly soon; classic reds will need considerable bottle-age.

1990★★ to ★★★★

A hot growing season. Moderate whites, better reds.

Drink whites now. Pinot Noir and Pinotage ready soon. Cabernets will benefit from bottle-age.

1989★★ to ★★★★

Passable whites, some very good reds.
Drink up whites. The softer reds pleasant now; Reserve quality Cabernets will develop well.

1988★★★★

A hot year, some very good wines: excellent Cabernet, Shiraz and new blended reds, some quite tannic, all with good fruit.
A vintage to buy and keep.

1987★ to ★★★★

Variable weather conditions and wines. Better for reds, but some notably good Rieslings and late-harvest wines.
Drink up dry whites. Cabernet and Pinot Noir drinking well but will keep.

1986★★ to ★★★★

An unusually hot and dry summer. A small crop of mediocre whites but good to excellent reds. Some good Chardonnays: a relatively new cultivar in the Cape.
Firm whites still drinking well, the late-harvest wines needing more bottle-age. Best reds lovely now but will keep.

1985★★ to ★★★

A cool summer and frequent rains resulted in variable quality, but good sugar/acid ratios. Overall, the whites were better than the reds, which tended to be light, and some excellent sparkling wines were made.
A year which saw much experimentation with new blends of classic European grape varieties.
Drink now.

1984★★ to ★★★

High temperatures during the harvest resulted in overripe whites with low acidity. A better vintage for red wines.
Drink up dry whites. 'Noble' late-harvest wines still superb. Top reds, such as Meerlust Rubicon, excellent with 10–20 years life ahead.

1983★★

A large crop of grapes, up on the 1982 record harvest but lacking sugar and acidity. Overall, moderate quality wines produced; yet some very good wines too: Zinfandel and Cabernet blends, and late-harvest whites.
Dry white too old; sweet possibly at zenith. Reds holding well.

1982★★★★

A very good year for reds, particularly Cabernets. The largest production of quality wines up to that time resulting from well-nigh perfect climatic conditions.
The best reds drinking perfectly and will probably keep on developing until, perhaps beyond, 2000.

1981** to ****

Cool weather from flowering to harvest time resulted in white wines of high fruit acidity. The reds were less good, soft and lacking colour.
Drink up.

1980* to ****

A hot, dry summer. The dry whites lacked acidity and were of moderate quality. A very good year for the reds. The Nederburg sweet white Edelkeur magnificent.
Dry whites passé. *Reds at peak.*

1970s

The 1970s was a decade of development: **1979**** the driest and warmest winter since the mid-1920s, autumn warm and wet resulting in much *Botrytis* and some very good late-harvest whites (Riesling and Chenin Blanc), also some good Pinotage; **1978**** good quantity and quality; **1977**** wet harvest, passable high acid whites, light reds; **1976**** almost ideal conditions, excellent reds, good whites, Edelkeur outstanding; **1975**** a large crop of average quality, low acid whites, rain-spoiled reds.
    1974*** a warm, very dry year; some excellent reds now passing their best. **1973**** cool vintage, small crop: Pinotage and Cabernet Sauvignon have held well; at peak. **1972** to **** a hot, dry vintage producing high quality reds, the best still holding well. **1971**** a large crop, relatively light wines, yet the reds can still be very good to drink. **1970****

1960s

Of the 1960s decade, **1969** and **1963** were the best vintages. The reds are now faded but they retain flavour and charm.

VINTAGE CHAMPAGNE

CHAMPAGNE HAS SOMETHING IN COMMON WITH port in that grapes are harvested and wine made every year but only in years producing wines of good to exceptional quality is it marketed as 'vintage'. Champagne is a blended wine usually, but not always, a blend of three different major grape varieties: Chardonnay, Pinot Noir and Pinot Meunier, each chosen for its different character. The grapes themselves are grown in different districts, some surprisingly far apart, but classified by quality. Most champagne is marketed under a brand name, no vintage stated. These non-vintage wines may, in turn, be of different years, blended by the chief taster to match his house style.

Non-vintage champagne varies in quality from passable to excellent, the best – Roederer for instance – benefiting from further bottle-ageing, and the top wines, such as Krug's Grande Réserve, being finer than many vintage champagnes.

However, a vintage champagne of one of the *grande marque* houses represents a level of quality superior to even its most successful bread-and-butter 'NV' brand. The proliferation of smartly dressed and high-priced *de luxe* champagnes are an up market ploy though they should, and mostly do, represent the highest and most refined quality of a major champagne house.

One just buys and drinks non-vintage champagne though, as stated above, some benefit from further bottle-age. Nine months rest in one's cellar can markedly improve a frothy young wine.

Straight vintage and *de luxe* vintage champagnes are not marketed until some five years or so after the vintage and, though most can be – and are – drunk within a couple of years, many benefit quite considerably from further bottle-ageing. Generally speaking vintage champagne is best drunk between five and 15 years after it was made, depending on the weight and style of the wine – and one's personal taste. I aim for an average of 12 years.

Old champagne has a peculiarly English appeal. After 20 years it gains colour and loses its pristine sparkle. Its bouquet and flavour becomes deeper and richer. If the bottles have been well cellared and the corks are firm, champagne can be delicious after 30, even 50 years and, if lacking effervescence, can be refreshed half and half with a young non-vintage wine, the young champagne providing zest and sparkle, the old wine character and flavour.

Older vintage champagne disgorged in the original cellars before shipment has a different character to bottles never recorked. Bollinger 'RD' is the best known: the date of disgorging/recorking usually on the back label. In my opinion all recently disgorged champagne should be drunk within a year or so after the RD date.

Lastly, do not hang on to, or pay high prices for, old vintages in half bottles, in jeroboams, or in larger sizes. Stick to bottles and magnums, the latter being best from the top champagne houses.

1991★★

What seems generally to be described as a useful year, in which an abundance of grapes helped stabilise prices and top up depleted non-vintage stocks.

The growing year started with early problems. Two spring frosts, the first in April destroying many of the buds, particularly in the valley of the Marne and the Côte des Blancs. The *grand cru* vineyards, particularly in the Montagne de Reims, were less affected. There was further frost damage overnight towards the end of May, mainly hitting the outlying districts of Aube and Aisne. However, when the weather improved a second wave of buds blossomed. Chardonnay flowering began uneasily around June 25 but weather brightened up a week later for the Pinot Noir and Meunier, ending July 10. Thereafter the grapes developed perfectly through a hot summer. However, on September 21 the weather suddenly deteriorated causing rot, though rain did help swell the grapes. The sun returned for a latish harvest beginning September 30.

The wines are light, with low acidity levels, not of *grand marque* vintage quality.

1990★★★★★

A potentially outstanding vintage, although many of the big houses are being very cautious in making any judgement. It was the third-largest vintage on record from the fifth successive above-average yield.

Following frost damage in April which affected some 45% of the total crop, sometimes dramatically, flowering was abundant but affected by unseasonable weather, resulting in *coulure* and *millerandage* in all grape varieties.

Summer in Champagne was typical of the rest of France: hot and dry, leading to a second flowering and thereby recouping as much as 60% of the crop, some of which was gathered at a second picking (the second such harvest in two years). Late summer rains and cool winds helped fill out the grapes while also having the effect of significantly increasing the potential alcohol. Both alcohol and acidity levels were excellent.

Most of the *grandes marques* will declare a 1990 vintage. *'For 45 years I have lived in Champagne, and never have I seen such a year'*, said Claude Taittinger, president of Champagne Taittinger. Some expressed doubt though: *'To say today that it is an exceptional year, that is wrong'*, said Bollinger's director, Christian Bizot after the harvest. For others, however, this was undoubtedly a great year, Henri Krug of Krug Champagne considers 1988, 1989 and 1990 as the outstanding trio of the century.

1989★★★★★

A large crop of superb quality. The grapes were grown and the wines made in perfect conditions, producing wines which rival 1982 for the title 'vintage of the decade'.

A warm spring was broken by frosts in late April. Conditions improved rapidly thereafter and flowering took place in late May. The summer was hot and sunny and produced luscious, healthy grapes ready for the harvest to begin on September 4 for Chardonnay and September 12 for the Pinots.

Quality apart, this was also an exceptional year due to there being two harvests, the second taking place in October, a rare event in Champagne. The second crop produced slightly acidic wines, suitable for blending.

Likely to be very appealing wines, tempting to drink early but, like the '76s, will gain depth and subtlety with bottle-age, 15 to 20 years not being excessive.

1988★★★★

A year which produced some very good champagne. The quantity was down 10% on the previous year, forcing the champagne houses to compete for grapes at a time of high world demand for the finished product.

A mild, frostless spring was followed by a good flowering in early June under perfect conditions. Progress was hampered by a cloudy July and heavy rainfall before the harvest, which began on September 19.

This vintage will be shipped only if demand, quality and quantity match.

Wait and see.

1987★

Unlikely to be a vintage year, but one which produced some very useful wines to stock up the cellars of the trade. A poor, wet summer resulted in some grey rot, but the crop was saved, in terms of quantity if not quality, by fine weather occurring during the harvest.

1986★★ to ★★★

Following a poor spring, flowering took place in late June under ideal conditions. The summer was hot and sunny, but rain during August and early September adversely affected the quality of the grapes.

This was a moderately good year except where growers did not successfully spray against rot.

The first 'vintage' wines of this year were launched onto the market in the summer of 1992.

Can be drunk now but the best will benefit from further bottle-age, say 1996–2000.

1985★★★★★

The severe winter, during which temperatures dropped as low as –25°C (–13°F), destroyed around 10% of the region's vines. In some areas as much as 25% of the vine area was destroyed.

Wet, dull weather conditions in spring and early summer eventually gave way to a sunny July. The months of September and October were the deciding factors *vis à vis* the quality of this vintage: delightfully warm, sunny weather swelled and ripened the grapes and the harvest took place late. The wines produced have the perfect balance of fruit character, alcohol and acidity.

Growers predicted a tiny production this year. They were pleasantly surprised by a small but excellent, stylish vintage for everyone. The best of the mid-1980s.

Beguiling now, particularly if you like your champagne at its liveliest, though classics like Veuve Clicquot, La Grande Dame and Roederer Brut and Cristal will improve over the next decade.

1984

A dull, wet spring led to a poor, late flowering. The weather did not improve during the summer and September rains caused rot. A non-vintage year.

1983★★★

Initially hailed as an excellent year throughout Champagne, the wines do not in fact merit such praise, but are mainly pleasant, flavoury and nicely balanced.

Good weather during spring and summer provided ideal growing conditions for the cultivation of a large crop of healthy grapes. September saw isolated patches of rain but October provided good harvesting conditions.

The amount of grapes needed for pressing one hectolitre of must was increased by the CIVC from 150 to 160kg, resulting in more concentrated wines.

Some assertive and potentially long-lasting wines, notably Dom Pérignon, Veuve Clicquot and the three Charles Heidsieck blends, Blanc des Millenaires, Brut and Champagne Charlie.

1982★★★★

A substantial vintage in every respect. With the exception of a bout of mildew in June and July, excellent conditions prevailed throughout the year. The grapes were ripe and healthy and rain shortly after the start of the harvest prevented them from over-ripening. The biggest crop on record.

Lovely when they first came on the market. This is an elegant, seductive year for vintage champagne. The best are still improving in bottle.

All delicious now but the heftier blends could do with more bottle-age: Dom Pérignon, Krug, Pol Roger Cuvée Winston Churchill and Roederer into the 21st century.

1981★★★

Difficult weather conditions cut the size of this vintage; it produced the smallest crop since 1978. Quality was very good.

A mild spring, which encouraged the early development of the buds, was followed by frosts in April and hail in May. The vines flowered during a cold July but the hot weather in August and September ripened the fruit well before rain in late September. Picking began September 28.

Most of the wine was used for blending, but many of the vintage champagnes have finesse, are firm and will last well.

Drink now, though Krug and the refined Cristal Brut will be delicious until the end of the 1990s.

1980★

The cold, wet weather in June and July led to a poor flowering which suffered from *millerandage*. Last-minute sun in September saved the vintage from disaster. A few champagne houses, including Krug, declared this a vintage, making pleasant wines; but on the whole very little vintage champagne was made, and wisely so. The wines were acidic and lacking body.

Drink up.

1979★★★★

An exceptionally cold winter which lasted through to April, followed by frosts in May; favourable conditions then continued throughout the summer and an abundant harvest of fully mature grapes was picked.

Stylish wines with the acidity to provide zing, zest and a long life.

In good, firm vintages like 1979 twelve years bottle-age is the yardstick, the best by then will be fully developed, the lesser wines past their prime, the heavyweight classics getting into their stride.

1978★★

The weather brought conditions close to disaster for the vines: a very small crop was produced.

Untypical wines.

Drink up.

1977

A dreary summer followed by better weather in September; the vines suffered mildew and grey rot.

Roederer Cristal Brut, made from highly selected grapes, about the only vintage '77 marketed. Drink up.

1976★★★★

The summer of great heat and drought. The harvest – the earliest since 1893 – began on September 1.

One of my favourite champagne vintages: firm, well-structured wines, the best will continue to give pleasure. The top vintage and de luxe champagnes will almost certainly improve further with age.

Krug and Dom Pérignon living up to their exalted reputation and good for another 10 years. Classic Pol Roger and Moët & Chandon delicious now.

1975★★★

After a wet winter, snow fell in March and the weather improved at the end of April. The summer was hot but not sunny and a slightly below average size crop was picked late. A good year: the wines tended to be a bit acidic but well-balanced, rounded and full of fruit and flavour.

Some lovely wines, notably Bollinger Brut, Lanson Red Label, Pol Roger Cuvée Winston Churchill, at or just passing their peak. Drink soon.

1974★

Difficult weather conditions. Variable wines, the best were not bad, but overall not really up to the standard of vintage champagne.

Drink up or avoid unless perfectly stored.

1973★★★

A very wet September followed a hot dry summer and produced an appealing vintage of fairly good quality. The wines had neither the body and flesh of the '70s, nor the lean firmness of the '71s, but were nevertheless enjoyable.

Mostly tired now, though the best champagnes are still pleasant to drink.

Despite some agreeable surprises, best to drink up.

1972

Not a vintage year due to a wet, sunless summer.

1971★★★★★

After spring frosts, June hail, August rain and even a tornado, September was mercifully hot and dry. A small crop of irregular grapes was picked. The wines were refreshing, lean, stylish and crisp. Champagne with finesse. The top wines can still be delightful to drink, the rest were at their peak from 1979 to the mid-1980s.
Drink up.

1970★★★★

After a cold spring and wet June, good growing conditions through to the harvest. Less shapely than the '71s but good, substantial wines – the best with time in hand.
All but the biggest of the classic grandes marques well past their best, but Bollinger Vieilles Vignes Francaises a good example of a magnificent stayer.

1969★★★

Moderately good. Unstable weather conditions and frequent violent storms during the summer. The worst mildew since 1958. The harvest began on October 1 in good conditions. Fragrant wines with a slightly higher than average acidity.
It is possible that this only moderately good vintage was released for two reasons: to make up for the two previous non-vintage years, and to supply an over-inflated market – though by its release in 1974, it had deflated.
At their prime in the late 1970s, early 1980s, only the top marques like Krug are more than just interesting.

1968

A disastrous year due to bad weather conditions.

1967

Vintage not declared due to disastrous harvest weather which caused widespread rot.

1966★★★★

A very good vintage. Some vines killed by harsh January frosts and then further damage caused by hail from May to August. An early June blossoming, some of which was damaged by a cold spell; August was wet with some mildew. The harvest took place in fine weather.
Despite the difficulties, 1966 produced a good quantity of firm, elegant, perfectly balanced, stylish champagnes.
One of my favourite vintages though, except for top wines like Bollinger and Cristal Brut, past their best. Drink up.

1965

Bad weather damaged crops; a poor year.

1964★★★★★

A first-class year which demonstrated how important it is to allow time in the bottle for big vintage champagne: the optimum time being 8–15 years or longer.

The vines enjoyed perfect weather conditions throughout the year. After a cold winter and early spring they flowered early, then ripened during a hot, dry summer. Gentle rain swelled the grapes during August, ready for an early harvest beginning on September 6.

Full-bodied, ripe and fruity champagne. Broader, riper and more rounded than the '61s and '62s though without the finesse of the former or the elegance of the latter.

The best, well kept, still drinking well despite depth of colour and loss of vigour. Salon le Mesnil superb.

1963

Appalling weather resulted in a poor, non-vintage year.

1962★★★★

Spring was cold and the summer was fine but lacked sun. The vines flowered rapidly but growth was hampered by cool temperatures. However, warm September sun ripened the grapes and the harvest began in conditions far better than expected in early October.

These were consistently good, dry, fruity, interesting wines. Still drinking well.

Best to drink up.

1961★★★★

A stormy April and cold May followed a mild, damp winter. Fortunately, the vines flowered in fine, sunny weather during June; after a cold July, good weather continued until the harvest on September 28.

A vintage which initially benefited from the popularity of the 1961 red Bordeaux, but also had its own merit. Still lovely, though some bottle variation.

No point in keeping longer though, at its best, kept well. Dom Pérignon is still one of the greatest ever champagnes produced.

1960★★

Not a vintage year, but welcomed by the trade who needed to stock up on non-vintage champagne.

1959★★★★★

An exceptional and timely vintage. Coming after a run of bad years 1959 was, at the time, thought to be the best for decades and is now mostly consumed.

The weather was wonderfully hot from May through to an excellent harvest. Well-constituted, ripe wines which held well for several decades.

The great, full-bodied, classic marques still make a lovely mouthful – if you like mature champagne. The rest need drinking up.

1955★★★★

A first-class vintage. Apart from a bout of May frost, good weather rallied throughout the year. Picking began on September 29 and reports noted an unusually high quality of juice from the grapes. This was an underrated vintage, the wines of which, if stored in cold cellars, can still be delightful. ·

Lovely wines, though past their best; drink up.

1953★★★★

Apart from a prolonged cold spell, the summer was satisfactory. Picking began early on September 14 and finished in very fine weather. 1953 was a highly satisfactory year. The wines were perhaps less firm and refined than the '52s, but overall, well-balanced and appealing. Very popular in the 1960s and 1970s.

Charming wines, now long past best. Few, understandably, remain, but worth looking out for.

1952★★★★★

Good weather conditions throughout the summer; then welcome rain fell in August and swelled the berries, causing only very limited rot. Extremely healthy grapes were harvested. This was a year of extensive variety, but overall producing firm, well-balanced, stylish champagnes. Still worth seeking out.

A better bet than the '53s, body and acidity keeping them well. Bollinger sheer perfection. Scarce. Delicious.

1949★★★★

A small crop which prompted cautious optimism after the harvest. After a long and difficult flowering, conditions improved with an exceptionally dry summer interspersed with occasional rain and hail. This was a very good year, producing firm, fruity, elegant wines. Many gained enormously from bottle-age.

Now straw-coloured and lacking effervescence, all at best lovely old wines. Depends on storage.

1947★★★★

A classic year. The vines flowered very early in June and then record hours of sunshine during August produced a small crop of wonderfully healthy grapes picked in ideal conditions. Despite their soft fruitiness, the wines have lasted well.

Drink up.

1945★★★★★

Bud-break was early, followed by April frosts and a difficult flowering. Picking began in haste on September 6 and yielded a very small crop of exceptionally high quality grapes. A long-lasting, elegant vintage.

If perfectly cellared, can be delicious.

1943★★★★

Low temperatures and frequent showers caused problems for the flowering. Vines were also attacked by oidium, particularly on the Côte des Blancs. This was however, a very good year: remarkable for being more successful than any other classic French district and, more importantly, for being the first major vintage to find its way into export markets after the war. Mainly drunk too young.

Over-the-hill now. Beware of '43s shipped in 1953 to celebrate the Coronation of HM Queen Elizabeth II. They should have been drunk at that time.

1942★★★

A good but little known wartime vintage.
Can still be good, but drink up.

1941★★

A moderately good, if rather light, wartime vintage. Rarely found these days.
Now: for those who like old champagne.

1930s

The 1930s saw four vintage years and six undeclared vintages of very poor quality.

1938★★ was the least successful of the declared years: the wines were of uneven quality, not shipped because of the war, and very few have been seen in England since. The previous year, 1937★★★★★ was, however, excellent – a vintage which turned out to be the highlight of the 1930s. These were rich wines with the acidity to give them a long life; some are still drinking well.

1934★★★★ enjoyed fine weather, healthy grapes and an abundant harvest. 1933★★★★ also benefited from very good conditions. The wines were reported at the time to be possibly the best of the century. However, the trade was more interested in those of 1934.

The first three years of the decade were menaced by appalling weather conditions and did not produce vintage champagne.

1920s

A decade which included many exceptional years. 1929★★★★ produced a large quantity of soft, charming wines but they were not of the same quality or as long-lasting as the outstanding '28s. 1928★★★★★ saw a fine summer following bad winter weather, and produced well-constituted wines which, if well kept, can still be excellent.

The next vintage year was 1926★★★ producing a small crop of good wines. Two non-vintage years followed, and a small crop of good quality wines was produced in 1923★★★★ the best of which were still excellent in the early 1970s and, if perfectly cellared, can still be lovely, golden-coloured with a hint of sparkle, and flavoury.

1921★★★★★ produced top-class wines despite difficult weather conditions. This year marked the peak of a great era for Clicquot and is probably the greatest white wine vintage this century. 1920★★★★ was subject to bad weather and mildew but enjoyed glorious harvesting conditions and was another very good vintage.

1910s

The 1910s witnessed several good years and one exceptional vintage.

1919★★★ produced refined wines, coming after three mediocre years. **1915★★★** was the next good vintage, the grapes were picked early by prisoners of war and soldiers on leave. Much of the Champagne district was under German occupation in **1914★★★★** a year which, nevertheless, produced some delightful, lively wines.

The best vintage of the decade was **1911★★★★★** – this probably the best since 1874. The weather was excellent and the harvest early. This year also endured Easter riots in the champagne industry.

1900s

Apart from three successful years, the 1900s was not a great decade.

1906★★★★ suffered a drought but produced a small quantity of very good wines. **1904★★★★★** enjoyed perfect weather and outstanding quality; the wines were lively and flavoury.

1900★★★★ gave an abundance of very good wines following a hot summer and storms in August. Phylloxera was meanwhile progressing through the vineyards.

Apart from these three years, this decade was menaced by torrential rain and disease, or, as was the case in 1907, a shortage of labour which resulted in a proportion of the crop being left to rot.

1890s

The 1890s revealed some good vintages. They included the excellent **1899★★★★★** and good **1898★★★** but not the poor and uneven period between 1897 and 1894.

1893★★★★ was harvested in late August – the earliest harvest ever. Much wine of very good quality was made, though the grapes were perhaps a little too ripe.

The finest vintage of the decade was **1892★★★★★** spring frosts reduced the crop by 25% but the harvest took place in perfect conditions. This year was also noted for the advent of phylloxera. The previous two years were not declared.

Pre 1890

The best vintages recorded: **1874**, fashionable and high-priced; **1868, 1865, 1857, 1846** and **1815**.

VINTAGE PORT

PORT, THE QUINTESSENTIAL 'ENGLISHMAN'S WINE' comes in several guises. In the old days, prior to 1960, there were 'wood ports' and 'vintage ports', all except for the white ports of the former category being sweet. White port, never popular in the United Kingdom, though delicious before lunch in a shippers' lodge or on a hot day up at a *quinta*, is made from white grapes and generally medium-dry. The other two wood ports took their names from their colour: 'ruby' being a lusty young wine, undergoing relatively little maturation in cask or vat, and true 'tawny' having lost its colour in cask, at the same time becoming softer, mellower, more nutty-flavoured.

Then there was the 'vintage port'. Up to 1970 shipped to the United Kingdom (and just a few other countries, Denmark for example) in 110-gallon (550-litre) 'pipes' and bottled two years after the vintage by the importer, by a wine merchant, or even, not uncommon in the 19th century, by the butler of a big house. Since 1970 all vintage port has had to be bottled by the shipper (the producer; the company owning the brand) in Vila Nova de Gaia (this commonly referred to as 'bottled in Oporto' though the lodges – warehouses where the port is matured – are all across the river Douro in Gaia).

Over the past few years the market has been greatly complicated by 'late bottled' vintage port (LBV) and, even more recently, by a rash of new 'single-quinta' wines. But the quality end is dominated by fine old tawnies, still woefully under appreciated, and the classic vintage ports, which represent the *crème de la crème*, the pinnacle of the port market.

The subject of this pocket book is vintages. Happily, despite some of the complications referred to above, port vintages are relatively easy to understand, to remember.

A vintage is 'declared' when circumstances are right: when the year in question has produced wines of the highest quality and, at the time of considering a declaration (normally after the next vintage), that the market is ready. For example, 1931, a great year, was not declared because of the depression in 1932/3. Life is made even simpler if the declaration is general, ie that the majority of the major shipping houses agree on quality and timing.

The only problem with vintage port is that it takes so long to mature and, though good value when first put on the market (compared with first-growth claret), requires capital to be tied up for considerable length of time, at least ten, often over 20 years. But at its zenith, it is the loveliest of wines.

1991★★★★

A very good year and likely to be 'declared' unless the saturated port market improves. Generally dry winter but very wet from January through to April though flowering took place in May in warm, dry weather. The summer hot and dry, the flower set excellent, but the heat and lack of rain resulted in thick skins and reduced flesh, though a sprinkling of rain September 10/11 helped, with more rain towards the end of th month swelling the berries. Mostly deep coloured, ripe wines which are looking promising.

'Vintage', if bottled in 1993, will need 10–20 years ageing, though doubtless good single-quinta and late-bottled port will be – should be – drinkable well before the end of the century.

1990★★★

Severe heat in July and August held back the ripening of some varieties; the Tinta Barocca grapes were particularly badly affected by *queima* or burning.

Picking began early, on September 3, but the maturity of these grapes was uneven. Instead of the super-ripe fruit that many growers had expected, sugar levels were frequently low and acidity too high; better grapes were, however, picked after overnight rain on September 19/20.

A huge quantity of high quality port would have been made but for a shortage of *aguardente*, or the brandy used to fortify the wine. As a result, many reputable growers were forced to make ordinary table wine from high quality must that would otherwise have been used to produce port. However, it has since transpired that the 'shortage' of brandy was actually due to the officially, yet not widely known, permitted over-production of port wine.

At the time of writing there are some excellent wines from 1990, undoubtedly of declared vintage quality. However, it seems unlikely that anyone will declare a vintage given the recession in the UK and the US – the two largest markets for vintage port.

Single-quinta or LBVs drinkable from about 1994 to, say, 1998.

1989★★

After a disastrous year, the port trade hoped that 1989 would produce a much needed abundance of good-quality wines suitable for blending. This was not to be. A summer-long drought yielded a small quantity of wines which showed good vintage potential.

A dry winter was followed by a hot, dry spring. Drought conditions prevailed throughout Portugal already, particularly in the eastern areas, except for a few very localised districts which saw rain and even the occasional hail storm in early summer, recurring later in August. Elsewhere the drought continued throughout the summer until the harvest (beginning on September 6) when rain swelled the grapes, and proved beneficial to growers who picked late.

The drought resulted in a small crop of rather dry grapes and as a result the wines tend to lack colour and balance. The best came from the central area of the port-making vineyards. Because of the 1988 shortfall of wines for standard blends, 1989 is unlikely to be declared.

Note regarding 'drinkability' irrelevant as this wine will be lost in ruby and tawny blends.

1988★★

A mild winter was followed by a cold, dry spring. The months from April to July were the wettest in 30 years, causing *coulure* during flowering and later mildew, reducing the crop considerably – by around 30–35%.

The wines were good but not of vintage quality. Meanwhile, the market was suffering from a severe shortage of wines suitable for use in blends.

Mainly due for blending, but Martinez and any single-quinta wines drinkable between 1996 and 2004.

1987★ to ★★★★

Had it not been so soon after the 1977 had been declared, 1987 would have qualified for 'vintage' status. Instead, apart from one or two single-quinta wines, declared only by Martinez. A mild, dry winter and warm, dry spring provided good conditions for a prolific and successful flowering. However, hopes for an abundant crop were marred by three months of uninterrupted drought and heat which produced small, dehydrated berries.

The harvest began as early as September 7 in some areas in scorching, arid conditions which broke on September 21 when rain swelled the remaining grapes. The wines made from these grapes were of better quality than those picked earlier, which were overripe and tended to lack acidity.

This was a bigger than average vintage of variable quality.
Some good single-quinta wines to drink now–1997.

1986★★

Not declared After a cold, wet winter a long, cold spring with frosts in April followed, and the weather did not warm up until early May. The vines were by now three weeks behind their normal growth schedule; matters were improved, however, by warm conditions during the first week of June which were perfect for flowering.

An uneven summer produced small, shrivelled grapes, then in the second two weeks of September heavy rainfall caused flooding in the Douro, 50mm (2 inches) of rain being recorded in one weekend at Pinhão. Warm weather followed, encouraging a rise in sugar levels and providing better conditions for the harvest.

In the Upper Douro a good quantity of grapes was gathered, but in the Lower Douro the wet weather returned in October and the grapes suffered from rot.
Some late-bottled vintage port of variable quality which ought to be drunk soon.

1985★★★★★

26 shippers declared An unquestionably attractive vintage, declared unanimously as a vintage year; almost, but not quite, of the calibre of 1945, 1963 and 1977.

An extremely wet winter and late spring retarded the growth of the vines by around two weeks. Some very localised areas saw severe thunder and hailstorms during the first days of June causing the loss of over a third of the crop. Elsewhere the summer was hot and extremely dry and the healthy but too-dry grapes were harvested from mid-September.

Some winemakers experienced difficulties during fermentation due to the very high temperatures and the wines lacked freshness and bouquet. Otherwise, a first-rate, vibrant vintage, concentrated and fruity.
Lovely wines, tempting to drink whilst young and fruity, but the classic shippers' should be kept for another 3 years and will develop beautifully, well into the 21st century.

1984★★

Not declared A cold, dry winter was followed by a wet spring. With the exception of very high temperatures in July the summer was cool. Conditions improved with a hot, dry September and the harvest began on September 24. Four days later rain came, followed by high winds which dried the grapes and minimised the risk of rot. The harvest was eventually completed under ideal conditions. The wet weather reduced sugar levels and a large quantity of grapes produced good, sound wines.

A blending year. Some variable single-quintas and LBVs. Drink up.

1983★★★★

Roughly 10 major shippers The third of a moderately good to very good trio of vintages, declared too close together and by no means generally, leading to some confusion.

A dry, very cold winter ran into a cool, wet, uneven spring which did not warm up until early June. The resulting *coulure* caused the loss of around 20% of the potential crop.

After an uneven summer, September temperatures rose to as high as 30°C (86°F) with a few localised rainstorms at the end of the month. The harvest – which was one of the latest on record – started on October 3 in the Upper Douro and October 10 in the Lower Douro.

The best wines came from the Upper Douro, they have good colour, flavour and bouquet, and some are even outstanding. They are overshadowed, though, by those of the 1985 vintage and will remain undervalued until the confused market has calmed down.

Minor shippers and quintas drink now; major shippers such as Graham and Taylor from now to 2015.

1982★★★ at best ★★★★

12 shippers declared Some big names, including Cockburn, Graham and Warre, were not among those declared, having more faith in the '83s.

A dry winter was followed by a mild spring and flowering took place in May in mainly warm, sunny weather. Hot, drought conditions prompted an early harvest, starting September 8, during which a light sprinkling of much needed rain freshened the grapes.

High temperatures during fermentation resulted in uneven quality and perhaps a lack of elegance, making this a currently underpriced vintage. The best wines, however, are full, firm and robust with good underlying fruitiness.

All can be drunk now but the relatively few top shippers, such as Croft, will keep well beyond 2000.

1981★

Not declared A winter drought and cool spring delayed the onset of flowering until early June. Extremely hot weather followed and growth was retarded further by the lack of moisture in the soil, resulting in a reduction of the potential size of the crop.

Heavy rain, storms and severe gales affected both the area around Oporto and the Douro and coincided with the harvest around the middle of September. They did, however, freshen the now dried-up grapes and cooled temperatures down. Eventually, the sun reappeared.

The best wines were made in the Lower Douro where the grapes were picked latest.

Some reasonable LBV ports and the rest used for blending. *Drink up.*

1980★★★

Widely declared A vintage which was thought by many to have come too soon after the superlative '77s and the originally well thought of '75s.

A wet winter was followed by a cold, wet spring which continued, unchanged, until flowering. The summer was hot with virtually no rainfall until September 20/21 when it rained heavily in most of the Douro. Sadly this was too late to improve the grapes, which were picked from September 22 onwards. In the Lower Douro, however, where picking started later, grapes did benefit from the rainfall and enabled the production of some good quality wines.

Overall, this was a small vintage which produced some extremely pleasant wines. Useful for drinking while waiting for the '77s and '85s to mature. Considered by the Symingtons as much underrated.

Most are delightful now, the top wines will develop further, at their peak either side of 2000.

1979★★

3 minor shippers declared A wet, unsettled spring was followed by drought which continued from June onwards and eventually broke with heavy rains in mid-September.

Drink up.

1978★★★

8 shippers declared A cold, wet spring was followed by a long drought from June to October. Heavy, coarse, full-bodied wines. A notable vintage mainly for the large number of single-quinta ports marketed.

Most at their peak now, exceptions being Ferreira, Graham's, Malvedos and, of course, Noval Nacional.

1977★★★★★★

20 shippers declared A great vintage in the classic mould. A cold, wet winter ran into a dreary spring and a cool summer which retarded the development of the vines, but the situation improved radically with a September heatwave. Grapes were picked from September 28 and were, with the exception of those picked late in wet weather, in perfect condition.

Although there was some anxiety that the 1977 vintage had come too soon after the previously declared year (1975), this was declared as a vintage unusually early – shippers were impressed by the fresh bouquet of the wines. Notably, Martinez, Noval and Cockburn did not ship the '77, a decision which they later regretted.

Generally, these were deep, consistently good quality wines. They will be worth keeping for the next century.

1995–2020, even beyond; well beyond for the top wines. The minor wines enjoyable now. Most will be reasonably mature from 1997–2010.

1976★

2 shippers declared Not a vintage year. A drought ran through winter, spring and summer and ended in late August. Heavy rains fell during the harvest in late September. A small quantity of pleasant wines appearing as single-quinta and LBVs.
Drink up.

1975★★

17 shippers declared A vintage which was welcomed by all (including shippers in Oporto where life was dominated by the revolution) and consequently was somewhat overrated when declared.

A wet winter was followed by a long, hot summer. Early September rain swelled the grapes, but bad weather at the end of the month caused some damage in the vineyards. It was doubtless the wet weather which prevented the 1975 vintage from living up to earlier expectations.

Most are, in fact, drinking very pleasantly now, and should be consumed before the '77s and the vintages of the early 1980s.

1974★

Not declared Grapes were ruined by heavy rain falling during the harvest. (Vargellas marketed, as were some single-quinta ports.)
Drink up.

1973

Not declared A rainy wet spring, hot summer and a wet, unsettled September produced the occasional good wine.
Rarely seen. Drink up.

1972★

3 shippers declared Heavy rainfall either side of heat and drought. Some flavoury wines, but generally not declared.
Drink up.

1971★

Not declared A late flowering and late harvest produced some nice wines for blending.

1970★★★★★

23 shippers declared A highly satisfactory and yet underrated vintage. Also significant for being the last year in which a port could be shipped in cask for bottling in the United Kingdom. After 1970 bottling at the shippers' own lodges was made mandatory.

The weather was perfectly conducive to a good vintage. After a cold, dry spring, an ideal summer followed and some beneficial September rain. The harvest took place in very good conditions.

Sound, healthy, well-constituted wines. Much sturdier than originally considered, and with plenty of life ahead of them. The more I taste and drink the '70s, the more impressed I am. Still worth looking out for for laying down, even after 20 years.

Minor shippers now–2000; major shippers 1995–2020.

1969

Not declared Bad weather conditions resulted in unripe wines.

Few seen. Drink up.

1968★★

Not declared Some nice wines; a year of LBVs and single-quintas.

Drink up.

1967★★

4 shippers declared Apart from a wet May, the summer was hot and dry. Rain in September swelled the grapes and the harvest took place under favourable conditions. Cockburn, Martinez, Sandeman and Noval declared this vintage rather than the 1966, whereas Graham and Taylor treated it as second-class. Those who declared misjudged the vintage and the market.

Drink soon.

1966★★★★★

20 shippers declared An attractive, elegant, well-balanced vintage.

A wet winter ran into a stormy May. July was hot but the grapes were protected from the sun by the unusually generous foliage. Some rain fell.

Overall, this was an appealing, well-constituted vintage which was underrated and undervalued but then upgraded in the 1980s. Some might even outlive the '63s.

Most are drinking beautifully now but have the balance to achieve fuller maturity in, say, 5–15 years.

1965★

Not declared Not a vintage year but there were nice, ripe wines nevertheless.

Drink soon.

1964★

Not declared Difficult weather conditions and a labour shortage caused by the illegal emigration of workers to France made this a problematic year.

Drink up.

1963★★★★★

25 shippers declared An outstanding vintage which was met with great acclaim.

A wet, snowy winter and spring ran right through to April; cold and rain lasted until mid-June but thereafter the weather was fine and dry. Picking took place in good conditions, following some beneficial September rain. A large quantity of vintage port was made.

Well-constituted, deep, elegant wines for long keeping; the best were Dow, Fonseca, Graham, Taylor and Warre.

Most are drinking perfectly now. Some of the original high flyers are showing a good deal of maturity. The top wines up to 2020 or thereabouts.

1962★★

Not declared Some good wines were made. Disastrous winter floods were followed by generally good weather in the summer months.

A great, classic year for Noval Nacional.

The Nacional 1995–2020, the rest drink now.

1961★★★

Not declared Some good wines. Undeclared largely because of its proximity to the 1958 and 1960 vintages. Some single-quinta wines and good, commercial late-bottled vintages were made.

Rarely seen but drinking well.

PRIOR TO 1960, ONLY DECLARED VINTAGE YEARS NOTED

1960★★★ to ★★★★

24 shippers declared A popular, overall satisfactory vintage. Apart from two months of rain during February and March, the weather conditions were ideal: fine, hot and dry. Heat and rain during the harvest caused some problems for subsequent fermentation.

Generally well-balanced, attractive wines.

All are fully mature now but will give pleasure up to, and the best beyond, the end of the century.

1958★★★

12 shippers declared A pleasant vintage of good, if light wines. Uneven weather conditions included a hot June with the highest rainfall since 1896. The most substantial port was the Martinez.

Drink now.

1955★★★★★

26 shippers declared A very successful year – the best of the post-war vintages prior to 1963 – and greatly welcomed by the shippers and the British merchants.

A heatwave throughout April and May, a good flowering, some beneficial rain during late May and June, and a hot August. Grapes harvested in good conditions.

Generally well-balanced and potentially long-lasting wines: Taylor's was a blockbuster when young but is simmering down now. Overall, this is my favourite vintage for current drinking.

Mainly perfection now but most have the fruit and body to continue gloriously well into the next century.

1954★★★

3 shippers declared A good vintage but not more widely declared due to the out and out success of the '55s. Rarely seen. Malvedos very good.

1950★★

13 shippers declared A generally satisfactory year weatherwise, but light, uneven wines.
Drink up.

1948★★★★ to ★★★★★

9 shippers declared A very good but partially by-passed year. Budding was early and the flowering healthy. However, intense heat throughout August reduced the size of the crop, thickened the grape skins, and concentrated and raised the sugar levels.

Deep, powerful, alcoholic port. Fonseca good, Graham excellent, Taylor outstanding, finer, even better than the 1945s.
Perfect now.

1947★★★★

11 shippers declared A very good, abundant year which helped replenish merchants' stocks. The summer was long, hot and dry with some welcome September rain. Picking began on September 22 in perfect conditions.
Fully mature; needs drinking.

1945★★★★★

22 shippers declared An outstanding vintage; one of the best of the century and certainly the best since 1935. All the port was bottled in Oporto. A very hot, very dry summer was followed by some September rain. Harvesting took place in great heat prompting anxiety over fermentation. Ultimately, the quality was superb but quantity small – insufficient to fill the war-depleted cellars.

Generally, a magnificent, firm, fruity and powerful vintage which at its best can still be superb, though some wines drying out. Graham outstanding.

1944★★★★

3 shippers declared Superb quality but shippers concentrated on the '45s. Rarely seen.

1942★★★

10 shippers declared A very good year which suffered wartime neglect. Not often seen. Generally good weather conditions with the exception of a stormy June.

1930s

The 1930s saw only two years in which vintages were declared, but there was, nevertheless, some very good port made in other years.

1935★★★★★ (15 shippers) Healthy, top quality grapes which were harvested in perfect conditions. The best were the Cockburn, Croft, Graham and Sandeman, and the most magnificent of all was the Taylor.

The quantity, however, was smaller than that of 1934★★★★ (12 shippers), which was the first widely declared year after the excellent 1927 vintage, and also one of my favourites: good, well-balanced, classic wines. Now rarely seen but still worth looking out for.

1931★★★★★ (3 shippers), though splendid, was not declared. The demand was low, the British market being in the depths of the recession, and cellars still full of '27s. There was, however, an abundance of good ports and this vintage was made famous by just one: the magnificent, deep, full-bodied Noval, the Everest of vintage ports.

1920s

This decade produced one classic vintage, two good vintages and a string of undeclared years which were disappointing to good in quality.

The classic year was 1927★★★★★ (30 shippers). After a difficult summer and autumn, conditions were transformed by ten days of fine weather during the harvest in October. This vintage coincided with the height of the port market. Some wines are now thin and 'spotty', others still magnificent – multi-dimensional.

1924★★★ (18 shippers) produced good quality port, the quantity, though, was small due to four months of drought ending with heavy rain in September. Overall, these are wines which are still keeping well.

Prior to this, two other vintages were declared during the 1930s. 1922★★★ (18 shippers), a sorely neglected year that produced a small quantity of lightish wines, similar in style to the '17s. 1920★★★★ (23 shippers), the first major vintage after 1912, which produced a small crop of good, robust, long-lasting wines, which, if well kept, can still be good.

1910s

A decade which included one classic vintage, one very good vintage and several mediocre years.

A light elegant vintage was produced in 1917★★★ (15 shippers), the port was smooth and attractive, but not substantial and is now very rarely seen.

The classic vintage of the decade was 1912★★★★★ (25 shippers). Apart from rain in September which delayed the harvesting, the summer weather was hot, and rich, now ethereal ports were produced. One of Taylor's greatest vintages, still drinking well.

1911★★★ was a 'coronation' vintage, shipped only by Sandeman. Still lovely when last tasted in 1964.

1900s

The 1900s produced three of the four great classic vintages prior to World War One, (the fourth being 1912). 1908★★★★★ (26 shippers), was initially darker and fuller bodied than 1904 and 1900, and maintained its depth throughout its life. Cockburn's famed and still magnificent.

1904★★★★ (25 shippers) was indeed a great vintage, but lighter than 1900, though they have kept very well. **1900**★★★★★ (22 shippers) was a year of exceptionally fine quality, though rarely seen now.

1890s

The 1890s saw several good vintages and one classic. **1899**★ (one shipper) was not among them.

Only seven shippers declared the **1897**★★★★ (known as 'The Royal Diamond Jubilee Year'). The port from this year was fortified with Scotch Whisky as all the brandy had been used for the 1896s.

1896★★★★ (24 shippers) was the great classic vintage of the decade, although now of variable quality, thinning and tired.

1894★★ (13 shippers) was a middling to good vintage and of better quality than **1892**★★ (10 shippers), a moderate year, which is now rarely seen. **1890**★★★ (20 shippers) produced tough, tannic wines.

OLDER VINTAGES

1887★★★ Queen Victoria's Golden Jubilee vintage, still good to drink, as are **1884**★★★★★ **1878**★★★★★ **1875**★★★★ **1870**★★★★★ **1863**★★★★★ **1851**★★★★ and **1847**★★★★★ (the greatest of the mid-19th century).

MADEIRA

AT FIRST SIGHT MADEIRA SEEMS AN UNLIKELY candidate for a vintage pocketbook. It is at one and the same time simple to understand – its basic grape styles being Sercial, Verdelho, Bual and Malmsey, in ascending order of sweetness* – and highly complex; once tasted easy to enjoy. It is a fortified wine. Its method of making resembles sherry in some respects, port in others. Unlike either it undergoes a heat treatment which gives it its inimitable 'tang'.

Most madeira is blended and marketed under a brand name. Fairly recently a leaf has been taken out of the port shippers' books, notably by Blandy and Cossart Gordon, by producing excellent ten-year-old blends of the major grape varieties. But the glory of madeira lies in its vintage and *solera* wines. Happily, both are still made, which bodes well for the future.

Madeira is a semi-tropical island in the Atlantic, off the coast of West Africa. Though there are weather variations, the climate is delightful all the year round. Vintage time is unusually long, from mid- to late August until early October, depending on the grape variety, and, in this spectacularly mountainous island, on the altitude of the vineyard.

The following are the best known shippers of vintage and *solera* wines: Barbeito, Blandy, Cossart Gordon, Henriques & Henriques, Leacock, Pereira d'Oliveira and Rutherford & Miles; and amongst the old vintages, Acciaioly and H M Borges.

'Vintage' madeira is a wine made from one named grape variety (they are never mixed) of one vintage, matured in cask. A '*solera*' madeira, also with a named grape, usually bears on the label the year the *solera* was started, the original wine being topped up with younger wine of the same grape and quality as the matured blend is drawn off. After sufficient maturation in cask an old madeira will be put into demijohns for an unspecified storage time until needed for bottling.

It is not always clear from the label, or from a stencilled bottle, whether a dated madeira is straight (unblended) vintage or *solera*. Although vintage madeira tends to command a higher price, old *solera* madeira is often the finer drink.

It might be imagined that Madeira's weather is as idyllic as its setting and that vintage variations would not exist. Not so. The decade of the 1980s catalogues many of the problems and some of the excesses. Add to this rampant inflation, exceeding 33 percent in 1984, the cost of importing essential materials, and it is a wonder that the price of madeira can be competitive. Indeed in the lower quality range it is not. Happily, the demand for high quality island-bottled wine is increasing, and it is in top blends and, I believe, vintage madeira that the future lies.

'When to drink?' In essence, madeira is ready for drinking as soon as it is put on the market; young vintages are not bottled for 'laying down'. It can safely be assumed that any vintage or *solera* wine from prior to 1970 will be mature and ready for consumption. Also, happily, madeira is virtually indestructable and old vintages will, with few exceptions, still be drinkable.

1991★★★

The 1991 vintage in madeira was of very good quality, the grapes being free of any disease. The resulting wines have

---

* Less frequently seen, the shy bearing Terrantez and Bastardo varieties. Both rich.

plenty of fruit and promise well for their future development.

Production was considerably greater than in 1990. In particular the Jardim da Serra area produced a much greater quantity of Sercial than for very many years. Additionally the production of Bual at Calheta is estimated to have more than doubled, thanks to the new plantings of the varietal to replace the former hybrid vines.

The months of June, July and August were notable for their fine weather and although some rain fell during the vintage, picking was barely affected and, as mentioned above, the grapes reached the winery in good condition.

1990★★★★★

A generally excellent vintage, particularly for the noble varieties. Picking commenced August 16 in the classic lower-lying districts of the south – Camara de Lobos and Campanario, famous for their Bual and Malmsey. The Sercial and Verdelho harvest on the north side of Madeira started during the first week of September. The weather was cool during picking with some rain, though this was accompanied by wind quickly drying the grapes which were generally in perfect condition with good sugar readings. Crop slightly smaller than 1989.

1989★★★

June and July very cold with haze affecting the higher vine-yards, all of which delayed development and reduced the crop potential – by as much as 50% in the southerly Camara de Lobos, Estreito and Campanario districts. Heat returned at the end of July and continued throughout August. Overall, however, the quality of grapes was good, and the size of the crop on the north of the island compensated for the shortfall in the south. Clearly some improvement in the growth and harvesting of the Sercial grapes: large bunches, potentially high alcohol.

1988★★★★

One of the best vintages of the decade, all the major grape varieties suitable for high quality blends and with true vintage potential. Well-nigh perfectly balanced climatic conditions, though June and July were cooler than usual, delaying development. However, the quality of a late harvest was high with well-filled grapes and subsequently high alcoholic content.

The vineyards of the northern part of the island, around Santana and Porto Moniz were particularly successful regarding quantity and quality; in the south the crop was somewhat reduced, especially from the higher vineyards affected by low cloud and mist.

A noticeable and notable increase in the production of *Vitis vinifera* on the island, thanks to the Regional Government's programme persuading smaller farmers to switch from hybrid and ungrafted vine varieties to the classic Madeira grape types.

1987★★★★

A satisfactory growing season. Rain, even snow on the higher ground during January and February. Beneficial spring rains and, despite strong winds in April and May, a satisfactory flowering.

The harvest was three weeks earlier than anticipated, commencing the second week in August and continuing on the higher vineyards until the end of September. There was generally neither wind nor rain during picking though towards the middle of September an easterly wind from the Sahara raised the temperatures to 38°C (100°F), causing problems during fermentation and necessitating cooling of the must. A substantial crop of good quality.

1986★★

A poor start to the year: cloud and rain between January and March, also much snow on the high ground – conditions which delayed the seasonal work in the vineyards. To compensate, the late budding and flowering missed damaging winds. Heavy rain fell in May and July. Happily, in contrast to some previous years, the farmers had appropriate facilities to treat the vines. Rain again during the harvest necessitated speedy picking. The net result was an abundant crop of moderate richness.

1985

One of the worst vintages, with regard to both quantity and quality, in living memory. Production one of the lowest on record since oidium and phylloxera swept the island in the mid-19th century.

Winter was cool, but torrential rain throughout the island caused considerable damage to vineyards: terracing and soil were washed away. Spring was cool and abnormally wet; high humidity during leaf break and flowering resulting in viral diseases and mildews, affecting the development of early shoots. The situation was compounded by farmers' reluctance to use expensive sprays on already damaged vines, being washed away as soon as they were applied. Flowering was late and, because of extremely humid conditions, uneven and often incomplete. June, July and August were hot but also with relatively high humidity causing the spread of mildew and rot. Picking was spasmodic, from the first week in September through to early October. Some farmers did not pick at all.

1984

Atrocious weather conditions with a harvest to match. Extremely heavy rainfall from late February and through March resulted in landslides and much crop damage. Terrace walls collapsed, soil was washed away together with essential minerals and nutrients. Pruning was interrupted by the rain and by the necessity to replace soil and repair walls.

Flowering was delayed 4–5 weeks and when it did begin (late April early May) there was a further period of high winds and torrential rain; also, in the north, severe hail damage. Damp, humid conditions persisted through to early July causing large areas of powdery mildew, against which such spraying as was employed was ineffective.

July, August and September were hot though often cloudy. The late and uneven ripening delayed the start of picking until September 15 in the lower vineyards of the south and as late as September 28 in the north: one of the latest vintages on record; indeed, in the higher vineyards planted with Sercial and Verdelho the harvest, such as it was, did not begin until the second week in October. Overall, production 40% less than normal, grapes with low sugar content, causing a severe stock problem.

1983★★★★★

An outstanding year. High quality wine of vintage quality and for top-class blends.

A fairly cold, prolonged winter which rested the dormant vines and discouraged premature growth, a problem on the island. Spring was cool and damp with mildew problems, but flowering, though late, was satisfactory. July and August were very hot, with scorching winds from the Sahara necessitating picking as early as August 10 in the lower southern vineyards of Camara de Lobos, the Bual and Verdelho having exceptionally high sugar readings. However, the Sercial crop was reduced by mildew, wind damage and late ripening. The small crop of Terrantez was of the highest quality and is being nurtured by the Madeira Wine Company to produce an outstanding vintage of this rare wine.

1982★★

An exceptionally mild and dry winter did not provide an adequate vegetative rest period, and the low temperatures of mid-April and May resulted in uneven and late flowering. The higher than normal rainfall in the early summer hampered development, causing some mildew damage. However, despite cooler temperatures than normal, the vintage weather was dry and though late – some 12 days later than normal in the south, 8 days late in the north – progressed well. Crop 15–18% down on previous vintages. Moderate quality.

1981★★★

An average sized harvest of good quality grapes. Winter was warm and dry, pleasant for tourists but not for vines. An equally pleasant, sunny and dry summer resulted in satisfactory though later than usual ripening. Grapes such as Sercial, grown on higher ground, did best.

1980★★★★

An unusually mild spring and warm summer free of damaging winds. Harvesting began on August 25 in the south coast vineyards and from September 8 in the north, yielding an above average crop of good quality grapes with higher than usual sugar content.

Particularly noticeable, and welcome, was the larger crop of European grafted vines following the Government-assisted conversion scheme – started in 1975 – from hybrids, wine from the latter only for island consumption. However, apart from inflation, running at very high levels ever since the revolution of 1974, interest rates at 18.25% since May 1978 made the necessary stock holding a great burden for the major shippers.

THE DECADE OF THE 1970s

Detailed weather statistics and quality ratings for this period either unavailable or unreliable.